Baby

Kari Cornell, Editor

Knits

from Around the World

*20 Heirloom Projects in a
Variety of Styles and Techniques*

**Creative Publishing
international**

First published in the United States of America by
Creative Publishing international, Inc., a member of
Quayside Publishing Group
400 First Avenue North
Suite 400
Minneapolis, MN 55401

1-800-328-3895
www.creativepub.com
visit www.craftside.typepad.com for a behind-the-scenes peek at our crafty world!

ISBN: 978-1-58923-789-6

10 9 8 7 6 5 4 3 2 1

Library of Congress Cataloging-in-Publication Data avaialable
Digital edition published 2013
eISBN: 978-1-61058-860-7

Photo on page 73 courtesy of Library of Congress.
Technical Editor: Charlotte Quiggle
Copy Editor: Betty Christiansen
Proofreader: Karen Ruth
Book Design: Laura H. Couallier, Laura Herrmann Design
Cover Design: Laura H. Couallier, Laura Herrmann Design
Illustrations: Karen Frisa
Photographs: Ray+Barber

Printed in China

Acknowledgments

•••

Many thanks to all of the talented designers who've contributed a pattern to this fun collection: Myra Arnold, Nora Bellows, Donna Druchunas, Candace Eisner Strick, Sue Flanders, Libby Johnson, Wendy J. Johnson, Kate Larson, Melissa Leapman, Elanor Lynn, Heather Ordover, Kristin Spurkland, and Nancy J. Thomas. Without your creative energy and hard work, there would be no book, and I thank you all for the great project ideas you've sent to me over the past several years. It's been great fun to work with each and every one of you. Thanks to technical editor extraordinaire Charlotte Quiggle, who endured everything under the sun during the course of this edit, but managed to hand over the finished files on schedule. Thanks also to copyeditor Betty Christiansen and to photographer Stephanie Rau of Rau+Barber. Down to the details, you make these books read well and look fantastic. Last but not least, I thank Linda Neubauer and Winnie Prentiss of Creative Publishing international. Without their help and guidance, this book would not have happened.

Contents

Introduction

by Donna Druchunas

For centuries, mothers around the world have wrapped their babies in soft, hand-knit clothing that they made themselves. In Europe during ancient and medieval times, infants were wrapped in swaddling clothes—large pieces of cloth pulled tightly around the baby's body to keep them virtually motionless. It was believed that a baby's limbs should be kept straight to prevent them from growing crookedly. Today's baby blankets likely hail from this time-honored tradition. The striking, but simple Shibori Blanket on page 117 and the pretty Spanish Lace Blanket on page 68, both made of soft, washable yarn, are the perfect size for cuddling a precious baby.

European babies and toddlers were often dressed in simple gowns, which were sometimes worn with a shirt underneath for extra warmth. The gowns were wide and long with a placket or slit at the neck to make it easy to slide the garment over the baby's head. Shirts were usually shorter and were worn as undergarments. Both garments often had extra-large hems that could be let down as the child grew. Traditional Japanese baby clothes wrapped around the child like a kimono, which eliminated the need to pull a garment over the infant's head. The loose fit also allowed babies to continue to wear the same garment as they grew. The Danish Aunt Anna Sweater on page 12 and the Baby Kimono Sweater on page 112 were both inspired by the simplicity of these early baby dressing gowns.

Many of the baby accessories commonly used today have their roots in the past. Bibs, for example, have been used at least as far back as the sixteenth century. The Turkish Bib design, found on page 120, features a traditional Turkish motif and is knit in a washable wool, making it both beautiful and functional.

Babies have always needed hats or bonnets to keep them warm. Medieval coifs were simple, plain caps that tied under the chin. During Victorian times, bonnets became very elaborate and were often knitted in lace or with beads as decoration. The Finnish cap on page 24 and the Sanquhar Bonnet on page 56 are both decorated with intricate colorwork and are sure to keep a baby cozy.

Victorian knitting books contained many patterns for both simple and elaborately knitted baby hats, booties, dresses, and blankets. Baby booties are perhaps the most popular knitted gift of all times. The French Baby Booties on page 62, with sweet cables running up the toe, are quick to knit and sure to please.

Whether you're looking for something simple or elaborate, a quick knit or an in-depth project in colorwork or texture, on these pages you'll find wonderful projects to wrap babies in comfy knitting from head to toe. Make something for your own baby, or work up a few lovely projects for gifts. Enjoy!

KNITS OF
Scandinavia

NORWAY.

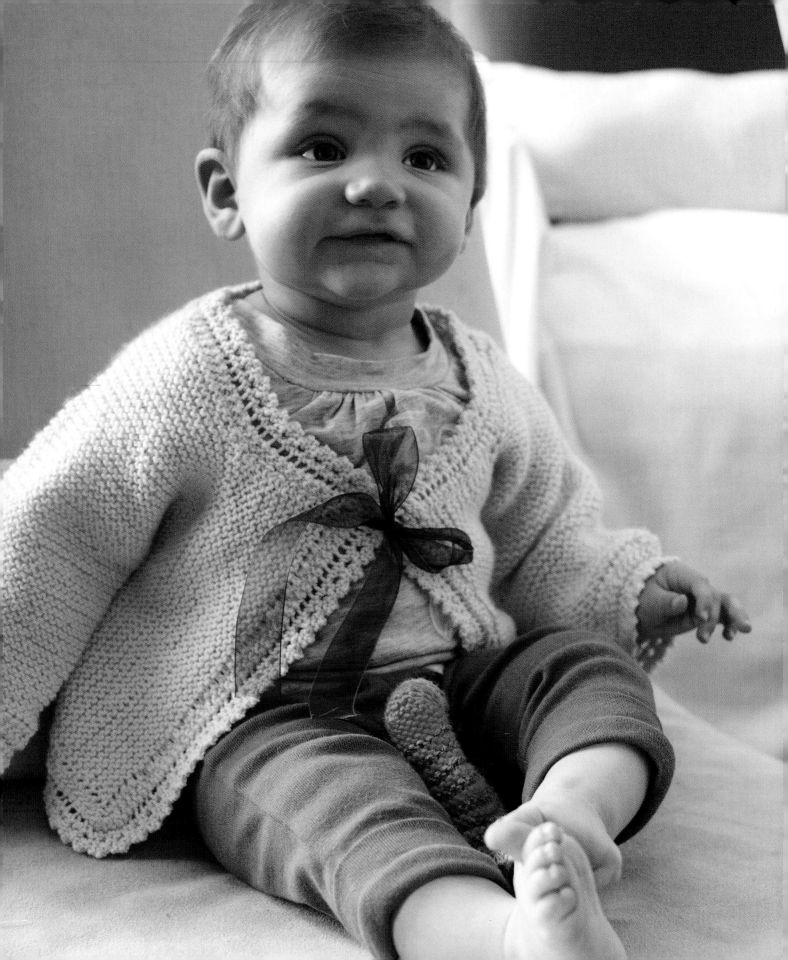

Danish Aunt Anna Sweater

•••

Traditional Aunt Anna blouses have been knit in all sizes for generations in Denmark. The sweaters were knit in unbleached cotton yarn, but this little sweater is knit in buttery-soft Koigu Premium Merino wool. The original sweaters were knit horizontally in garter stitch with an applied lace edging. Baby sweaters were worn with the buttons up the back. For this version, pretty ribbon bows close the front.

Design by Candace Eisner Strick

Sizes
9 (12, 18) months

Finished Measurements
Chest: 17½ (19½, 21½)"/44.5 (49.5, 54.5)cm
Length (including edging): 9½ (11¼, 13)"/24 (28.5, 33)cm

Materials
 Koigu KPM (fingering weight; 100% wool; 175 yds/162m per 1¾ oz/50g skein): 3 (3, 4) skeins Natural #0000

Size 0 (2mm) needles
Size 4 (3.5mm) needles or size needed to obtain gauge
Stitch markers
Tapestry needle
1 yd/1m ribbon

Gauge
23 sts and 42 rows = 4"/10cm in garter st with larger needles.
Adjust needle size as necessary to obtain correct gauge.

Pattern Notes

The sweater is worked cuff-to-cuff in garter stitch. When the sweater is finished, a lace edging is applied all the way around the body and cuffs. Ribbon is used in place of buttons to keep the front closed.

Slip first stitch of every row purlwise with yarn in front.

Pattern Stitch

Edging

Row 1 (WS): K1, k2tog, yo twice, k2tog, yo twice, k2—9 sts.

Row 2 (RS): K2, [(k1, p1) into double yo, k1] twice, k1; pick up and knit 1 st in edge of sweater, pass last edging st over picked-up st to join edging to sweater—9 sts.

Row 3: K1, k2tog, yo twice, k2tog, k4—9 sts.

Row 4: BO 2 sts, k3 (including st already on needle after BO), (p1, k1) into double yo, k1; pick up and knit 1 st in edge of sweater, pass last edging st over picked-up st to join edging to sweater—7 sts.

Rep Rows 1–4 for pat.

••• Instructions

Left Sleeve

With larger needles, CO 39 (45, 51) sts.

Slipping first st of every row pwise wyif throughout (see Pattern Notes), knit 7 rows.

Inc row (RS): Sl 1, kfb, knit to last 2 sts, kfb, k1—2 sts inc'd.

Rep Inc row every 8 rows 5 (6, 7) more times—51 (59, 67) sts.

Work even until sleeve measures 6½ (7½, 8½)"/16.5 (19, 21.5)cm, ending with a RS row.

Body

CO 24 (30, 36) sts at beg of next 2 rows for left front and back—99 (119, 139) sts.

Knit 18 (22, 22) rows, ending with a RS row.

Left Front

Next row (WS): K43 (53, 63) sts for back, BO 23 sts for neck, k33 (43, 53) left front sts; transfer back sts to holder or waste yarn.

Working on front sts only, work even until front measures 3¼ (4, 4½)"/8.5 (10, 11.5)cm, ending with a WS row BO.

Back

Transfer back sts from holder to needle; rejoin yarn at neck edge with RS facing.

Knit 50 (56, 66) rows and at end of last (WS) row, CO 23 sts—66 (76, 86) sts.

Leave sts on needle; do not cut yarn.

Right Front

With new ball of yarn, CO 33 (43, 53) sts.

Work even until right front measures same as left front neck, ending with a RS row.

Cut yarn; turn.

Body

With the WS facing, the back sts are on the RH needle and the yarn is attached to the last st.

Next row (WS): Join the sts of right front and back as follows: Using the yarn attached to the back, knit across the right front sts to complete the row— 99 (119, 139) sts.

Knit 18 (22, 22) rows, ending with a WS row.

BO 24 (30, 36) sts at beg of next 2 rows— 51 (59, 67) sts.

Right Sleeve

Knit 10 (12, 14) rows.

Dec row (RS): Sl 1, k2tog, knit to last 3 sts, ssk, k1—2 sts dec'd.

Rep Dec row every 8 rows 5 (6, 7) more times— 51 (59, 67) sts.

Work even until sleeve measures 6½ (7½, 8½)"/16.5 (19, 21.5)cm, ending with a WS row.

BO all sts.

Finishing

Sleeve Edging

Notes: Edging is worked perpendicularly to lower edge of sleeve and is joined to sleeve at end of RS rows. When picking up sts in sleeve edge, pick up 1 st in each CO/BO st.

With smaller needles, CO 7 sts.

Work Edging pat, joining to sleeve edge; continue until edging has been joined to entire sleeve edge.

BO all sts on WS.

Rep on other sleeve.

Sew right side and sleeve seams.

Body Edging

Note: Edging is worked all around body and neck of sweater in one continuous piece, beginning and ending at open left side seam. When picking up sts in sweater edge, pick up 1 st in each CO, BO st, or slipped st.

With smaller needles, CO 7 sts.

Work Edging pat, joining to sweater edge beg at open left side; work across lower back and right front. Turn lower right front corner by working 8 rows of Edging without joining to sweater. Continue up right front, around neck, and down left front, joining edging on each row of neck corners. Turn lower left front corner by working 8 rows of Edging without joining to sweater. Continue across lower left front to end.

BO all sts on WS.

Sew left side and sleeve seams.

Steam lightly.

Cut 6 pieces of ribbon 5"/12.5cm long. Sew 3 pieces of ribbon to WS of left front, spacing them as desired. Rep on right front, matching positions. Weave ends of ribbons through the yarn over openings so that they are on the RS. Tie in a bow to close cardigan.

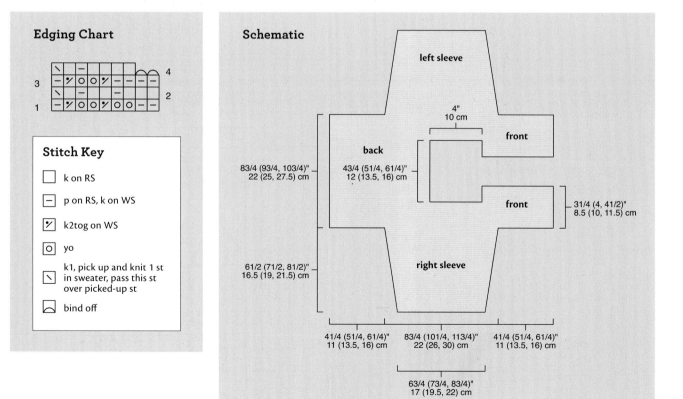

Edging Chart

Stitch Key

☐ k on RS

– p on RS, k on WS

↗ k2tog on WS

○ yo

↘ k1, pick up and knit 1 st in sweater, pass this st over picked-up st

⌒ bind off

Schematic

left sleeve

4"
10 cm

back

front

83/4 (93/4, 103/4)"
22 (25, 27.5) cm

43/4 (51/4, 61/4)"
12 (13.5, 16) cm

front

31/4 (4, 41/2)"
8.5 (10, 11.5) cm

61/2 (71/2, 81/2)"
16.5 (19, 21.5) cm

right sleeve

41/4 (51/4, 61/4)"
11 (13.5, 16) cm

83/4 (101/4, 113/4)"
22 (26, 30) cm

41/4 (51/4, 61/4)"
11 (13.5, 16) cm

63/4 (73/4, 83/4)"
17 (19.5, 22) cm

Faeroese Blanket and Hat

•••

The cat motif featured in this hat and blanket set comes from the Faeroe Islands; the colors were inspired by photos of farmhouses on the Faeroese coastline. The blanket is worked in the round, then cut open to lie flat. A fabric lining covers the cut edge and the floats on the wrong side of the work.

Designs by Kristin Spurkland

BLANKET

Size
One size

Finished Measurements
29" × 29"/73.75cm × 73.75cm

Materials

 Quince & Co *Lark* (worsted weight; 100% American wool; 134 yds/123m per 1¾ oz/50g skein): 5 skeins Pomegranate (A), 1 skein each of Petal (B), Glacier (C), and Leek (D)

Size 6 (4mm) double-pointed and circular needles (24"/60cm or longer)

Size 8 (5mm) double-pointed and circular needles (24"/60cm or longer) or size needed to obtain gauge

Stitch marker

Tapestry needle

30" × 30"/76cm × 76cm square of fabric

Sewing machine

Sewing needle

Sewing thread to match blanket or lining

HAT

Size
Newborn (12, 18, 36) months

Finished Measurements
Circumference: 14 (15½, 16¾, 18)"/38 (39.5, 42.5, 46)cm

Materials

 Quince & Co *Lark* (worsted weight; 100% American wool; 134 yds/123m per 1¾ oz/50g skein): 1 skein each of Pomegranate (A), Petal (B), Glacier (C), and Leek (D)

Size 6 (4mm) double-pointed and circular needles (24"/60cm or longer)

Size 8 (5mm) double-pointed and circular needles (24"/60cm or longer) or size needed to obtain gauge

Stitch marker

Tapestry needle

Sewing needle

Gauge for Blanket and Hat

20 sts and 22 rnds = 4"/10cm in stranded 2-color St st with larger needle.

Adjust needle size as necessary to obtain correct gauge.

Pattern Note

Work steek stitches as follows: On 2-color rounds, the steek stitches should be worked in a "salt and pepper" pattern, alternating 1 stitch of A with 1 stitch of the contrast color. On 1-color rounds, all steek stitches are worked with A.

••• Blanket Instructions

Lower Border

With smaller needle and A, CO 144 sts. Do not join in the round.

Rows 1 (WS), 4 and 5: K1, *k2, p2; rep from * to last 3 sts, k3.

Rows 2 (RS), 3 and 6: P1, *p2, k2; rep from * to last 3 sts, p3.

Do not turn work at the end of Row 6.

Body

Establish steek: CO 3 sts onto RH needle, pm for beg of rnd, CO 4 sts; join to work in the round.

Rnd 1: Change to larger circular needle; knit around and inc 1 st—145 blanket sts, 7 steek sts.

Work 24-rnd Blanket Chart 7 times, maintaining salt-and-pepper pat in steek section (see Pattern Notes), ending last rnd at beg of steek.

Next rnd: With A, BO 7 steek sts, knit around and dec 1 st; turn—144 sts.

Upper Border

Change to smaller needle and rep 6-row Lower Border pat.

BO all sts, working the knits and purls as they appear.

Cut Steek

With a smooth contrast-color yarn, hand-baste a line of stitches down the center of the 4th st of the steek. This marks the cutting line.

Machine stitch between the first and 2nd sts of the steek, then between the 6th and 7th sts of the steek.

Cut blanket open along cutting line (center of 4th st).

Wash and block blanket, blocking cut edges of steek so that they fold to the WS.

Weave in ends along cut edge.

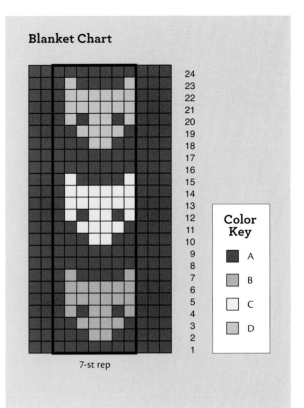

Blanket Chart

24 23 22 21 20 19 18 17 16 15 14 13 12 11 10 9 8 7 6 5 4 3 2 1

Color Key

- A
- B
- C
- D

7-st rep

Side Borders

With RS facing, using smaller needle and A, pick up and knit 146 sts along side edge.

Rows 1 (WS), 4 and 5: P2, *k2, p2; rep from * to end.

Rows 2 (RS), 3 and 6: K2, *p2, k2; rep from * to end.

BO all sts, working the knits and purls as they appear.

Weave in remaining ends.

Lining

Pre-shrink the fabric before lining the blanket.

Cut fabric to the size of the finished blanket.

Fold fabric edges under ½"/1.25 cm all the way around and press folded edges into place.

Pin fabric to WS of blanket, and hand stitch into place using sewing needle and thread.

••• Hat Instructions

With smaller dpns and D, CO 70 (76, 84, 90) sts. Distribute sts evenly around dpns, mark beg of rnd and join, being careful not to twist sts.

Work in p1, k1 rib for 2"/5cm.

Next rnd: [Yo, k2tog] around.

Next rnd: Knit.

Next rnd: Change to larger circular needle and A; knit around and inc 0 (1, 0, 1) st(s)—70 (77, 84, 91 sts).

Work 29-rnd Hat Chart.

With A, knit 0 (0, 0, 5) rnds.

Crown

Rnd 1: *K11 (13, 19, 28), k2tog; rep from * to last 4 (2, 0, 1) sts, knit to end —64 (72, 80, 88) sts.

Rnd 2: Knit.

Rnd 3: *K2, k2tog; rep from * around—48 (54, 60, 66) sts.

Rnd 4: Knit.

Rnd 5: *K1, k2tog; rep from * around—32 (36, 40, 44) sts.

Rnd 6: Knit.

Rnd 7: K2tog around—16 (18, 20, 22) sts.

Rnd 8: K2tog around—8 (9, 10, 11) sts.

Rnd 9: [K2tog] 4 (4, 5, 5) times, k0 (1, 0, 1)—4 (5, 5, 6) sts.

Cut yarn, leaving a 6"/15cm tail. Thread tail through rem sts, pull tight, then weave in end on WS to secure.

Weave in ends.

Hat Chart

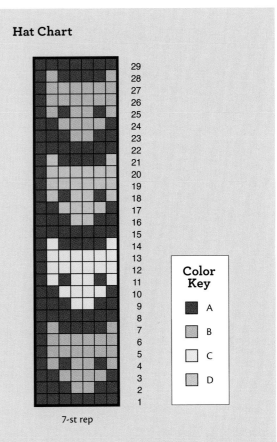

7-st rep

Color Key

■	A
■	B
□	C
■	D

Päivätär Bonnet and Mittens

• • •

Päivätär is the sun goddess in the Finnish epic poem *The Kalevala*.
Not only was Päivätär a goddess—she was the goddess of spinning, and her
sister, goddess of the moon, was in charge of weaving. The patterns in this
baby set have been used in both Finnish knitting and weaving.

Designs by Heather Ordover

Sizes
Mitts: 0–3 (6–12, 18) months
Bonnet: Newborn

Finished Measurements
Mitts circumference: 5 (6, 7½)"/12.5
(15, 19)cm
Bonnet (measured along front edge):
11"/28cm

Materials
1 Knit Picks *Stroll Sock* (fingering
weight; 75% superwash merino
wool, 25% nylon; 231 yds/211m per 1¾ oz/
50g skein): 1 skein each White #26082 (A),
Firecracker Heather #24587 (B), and Forest
Heather #24589 (C) for set

Size 2 (2.75mm) double-pointed needles
or size needed to obtain gauge (mitts)

Size 2 (2.75mm) 24"/60cm (or longer)
circular needle or size needed to obtain
gauge (bonnet)

Size 3 (3.25mm) double-pointed needles
(mitts)

Stitch markers

Stitch holder (bonnet)

Tapestry needle

Gauge
34 sts and 36 rnds = 4"/10cm in 2-color
stranded St st with smaller needles.
*Adjust needle size as necessary to obtain
correct gauge.*

Special Abbreviation

Slip marker (sm): Slip marker from LH to RN needle.

Pattern Notes

The charts show the three main motifs: a girl, a boy, and a snowflake. These can be interchanged easily (the girl and boy are both 10-stitch motifs; the snowflake is 13 stitches, making it easy to center over a central stitch). The Small sample shows the girl motif, the Medium sample shows the boy motif, and the Large sample shows the snowflake. You will need to made adjustments to the placement of the colored speckles surrounding the snowflake motif if using it in a Small or Medium.

If you wish to add a decorative ribbon to help keep the mitts on busy little hands, insert an eyelet round of [yo, k2tog] in charted Rnd 2. Thread thin ribbon or yarn through the eyelets and tie.

Also included is an alternate 13-round chart for another traditional cuff pattern if you want a longer mitt. It would replace the 8-round 2-color cuff.

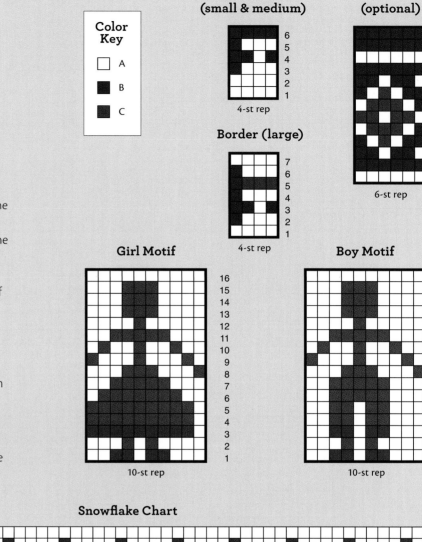

Color Key

☐ A
■ B
■ C

Border (small & medium)

4-st rep

Border (large)

4-st rep

Cuff Chart (optional)

6-st rep

Girl Motif

10-st rep

Boy Motif

10-st rep

Snowflake Chart

60 sts

13-st motif

Top

Rnd 1: With A, [k8, k2tog] 4 (5, 6) times around—36 (45, 54) sts.

Rnd 2: Knit.

Rnd 3: [K3, k2tog, k2, k2tog] 4 (5, 6) times around—28 (35, 42) sts.

Rnd 4: Knit. (For shorter mitt, skip to Finishing after completing this rnd.)

Rnd 5: [K2, k2tog, k1, k2tog] 4 (5, 6) times around—20 (25, 30) sts.

Rnd 6: Knit. (This is last rnd for Small)

Rnd 7 (Medium only): K3, k2tog, [k1, k2tog twice] 4 times—16 sts.

Rnd 7 (Large only): [K1, k2tog twice] 6 times—18 sts.

Finishing

Cut yarn, leaving a 12"/30cm tail.

Arrange sts evenly on 2 dpns so one of the motifs is centered on one of the dpns for back of hand.

Graft the sts tog using Kitchener st.

Weave in ends. Wash and block lightly.

••• Mitten Instructions

Cuff

Using larger dpns and long-tail method, with A over thumb and B over index finger, loosely CO 24 (34, 44) sts. Mark beg of rnd and join, taking care not to twist sts.

Work 8 rnds of k1A, k1B around.

Switch to smaller dpns.

Body

Next rnd: With A, [k2, kfb] 8 (11, 14) times, knit to end—36 (45, 58) sts.

Next rnd: Knit and inc 4 (3, 2) sts evenly around—40 (48, 60) sts.

Work 6-rnd (6-rnd, 7-rnd) Border Chart and, on last rnd, inc 0 (2, 0) sts evenly around—40 (50, 60) sts.

Work desired motif chart (Girl or Boy for any of the sizes; Snowflake for size Large only, see Pattern Notes).

Pattern Notes

The patterned front of the bonnet is worked first, then the back is shaped using a method similar to turning a sock heel.

The cap is sized for a newborn, but can be made larger for older babies. Measure from the lower edge of one side of the jaw over the top of the head and down to the other lower edge of the jaw. Multiply by gauge and use graph paper to chart the expansion of the pattern. Move the markers in set-up row out by 3 sts for each inch of added width. Then continue the bonnet construction with the new marker placement, adjusting row count as necessary.

Bonnet Chart

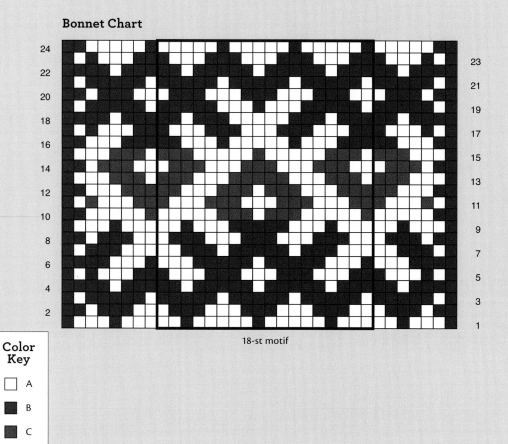

18-st motif

Color Key

☐ A

■ B

■ C

••• Bonnet Instructions

Plaited Edging and Front Panel

Using circular needle and long-tail method, with A over thumb and B over index finger, loosely CO 87 sts.

Row 1 (RS): K1A, *k1B, k1A; rep from * to end.

Row 2 (WS): K1A, [bring B *under* A, K1B; bring A *under* B, k1A]. Continue alternating colors, always bringing new color *under* the yarn used before.

Row 3 (RS): P1A, [bring B *under* A, p1 B; bring A *under* B, k1A]. Continue alternating colors, always bringing new color *under* the yarn used before.

Row 4: Rep Row 2.

Next 24 rows: Work Bonnet Chart. Cut B.

Note: For Rows 10–15, work the red edge sts using separate strands of yarn (intarsia-style); do not carry B all the way across.

Shape Sides

Row 1 (set-up, RS): With A, sl 1, k31, pm, k7, kfb twice, k2, (k1, p1, k1) all in 1 st, k2, kfb twice, k7, pm, k32—93 sts, with 29 center sts between markers.

Row 2: Slipping markers, sl 1, purl to end.

Row 3: Sl 1, knit to marker, sm, k7, kfb, k6, (k1, p1, k1) all in 1 st, k6, kfb, k7, sm, knit to end—97 sts with 33 center sts.

Row 4: Sl 1, purl to end.

Row 5: Sl 1, knit to 2nd marker, ssk, turn, leaving 30 sts unworked.

Row 6: Sl 1, purl to 2nd marker, p2tog, purl to end.

Row 7: Sl 1, knit to 2nd marker, ssk, knit to end.

Row 8: Sl 1, purl to 2nd marker, p2tog, turn, leaving 29 sts unworked.

Row 9: Sl 1, knit to 2nd marker, ssk, turn, leaving 28 sts unworked.

Row 10: Sl 1, purl to 2nd marker, p2tog, turn, leaving 28 sts unworked.

Rep [Rows 9 and 10] 14 times—14 unworked sts on each side.

Shape Center Back

Row 1 (RS): Sl 1, knit to marker, sm, k14, k2tog, k1, pm for center, ssk, knit to marker, sm, ssk, turn—31 sts rem in center.

Row 2: Sl1, purl to side marker, p2tog, turn—13 sts unworked each side.

Row 3: Sl 1, knit to marker, sm, knit to 3 sts before center marker, k2tog, k1, sm, ssk, knit to marker, sm, ssk, turn—29 sts rem in center.

Continue to dec at sides and rep Row 3 [every RS row] 3 more times—23 center sts.

Continue to dec at sides and work center even until 5 sts rem unworked each side.

Continue to dec at sides and rep Row 3 [every RS row] 4 times—15 center sts.

Work 2 more rows, dec at sides only—no sts rem unworked, 17 sts rem.

Move sts to spare dpn.

I-Cord Ties and Trim

With RS facing and using B, pick up and knit 20 sts along left side, k17 from dpn, pick up and knit 20 sts along right side—57 sts.

Purl across. Cut yarn and set aside.

With dpn and B, CO 3 sts. Work I-cord as follows: *K3, do not turn, slip sts back to LH needle; rep from * until cord measures 5"/12.5cm or desired length for tie.

Continue, working I-cord BO across back sts as follows: *K2, ssk (joining 1 I-cord st with 1 bonnet st), do not turn. Slip sts back to LH needle; rep from * until all live sts are bound off.

Continue working I-cord until tie measures same as for other side.

BO. Weave in ends. Block lightly.

Lofoten Island Sweater

•••

Cod fishing on the Lofoten Islands of northern Norway provided the inspiration
for this infant sweater that features a fishtail pattern on the bottom, fishnet
and waves on the body, and Codfish drying on racks on the yoke. It is knit
in the traditional Norwegian style—in the round with a steek for the sleeve,
which is sewn and cut later to make the armhole.

Design by Sue Flanders

Sizes
6 (9, 12, 18, 24) months

Finished Measurements
Chest: 18½ (19½, 20¼, 21¼, 22¼)"/27 (49.5,
51.5, 54, 56.5)cm
Length: 11¼ (11¾, 12¼, 12¼, 12¾)"/28.5 (30,
31, 31, 32.5)cm

Materials
3 Knit Picks *Swish DK* (DK weight;
100% superwash merino wool; 120
yds/131m per 1¾ oz/50g skein): 2 (2, 2, 3, 3)
skeins Dove Heather (A), 2 (3, 3, 4, 4) skeins
Twilight (B), 1 skein Dusk (C)

Size 4 (3.5mm) double-pointed and
16"/40cm circular needles or size needed to
obtain gauge

Stitch markers

Waste yarn or stitch holders

Tapestry needle

Sewing machine

Gauge
26 sts and 28 rnds = 4"/10cm in stranded
2-color St st.
*Adjust needle size as necessary to obtain
correct gauge.*

Special Technique

3-needle bind-off: With RS tog and needles parallel, using a 3rd needle, knit tog a st from the front needle with 1 from the back. *Knit tog a st from the front and back needles, and slip the first st over the 2nd to bind off. Rep from * across, then fasten off last st.

Pattern Notes

The body is worked in-the-round, from the bottom up.

5 extra steek stitches are added between the front and back for the armholes. Work the steek stitches as follows: K2A, k1CC, k2A, where CC is either B or C depending on the pattern round being worked. (On single-color round, work with whatever color is being used.) The steek stitches are sewn with a sewing machine and then cut to make the armhole openings.

The neck is shaped after the sweater is worked by machine stitching a curved line at center front, then cutting out the fabric inside the machine stitching.

Dotted lines on schematics show cut edges. All cut edges have facings covering them.

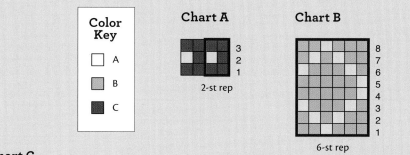

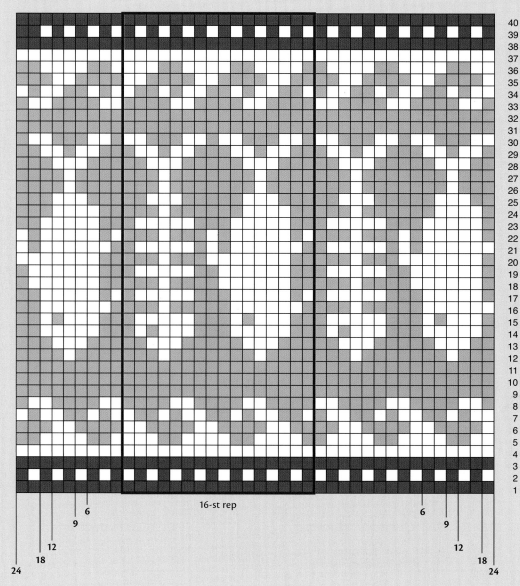

••• Instructions

Body

With smaller circular needle and C, CO 120 (126, 132, 138, 144) sts. Pm for beg of rnd and join, taking care not to twist sts.

Work Fishtail pat as follows:

Rnds 1–3: With C, *k2, yo, k2, k2tog; rep from * around.

Rnds 4–7: With B, *k2, yo, k2, k2tog; rep from * around.

Rnds 8–11: With A, *k2, yo, k2, k2tog; rep from * around.

Rnds 12–15: Rep Rnds 4-7.

Rnd 16: With C, knit around.

Work 3-rnd Chart A.

Work 8-rnd Chart B until piece measures 5½ (6, 6½, 6½, 7)"/14 (15.25, 16.5, 16.5, 17.75)cm, ending after Rnd 4 or 8.

Yoke

Rnd 1 (establish steeks): *With C, CO 5 sts for underarm steek; beg where indicated for your size, work 60 (63, 66, 69, 72) front sts following Chart C; rep from * for back.

Continue working Chart C and steek sts until 40-rnd chart is complete.

Thread all sts onto waste yarn.

Sleeves

With dpns and B, CO 36 sts; mark beg of rnd and join, taking care not to twist sts.

Work 16-rnd Fishtail pat as for Body, and on last rnd, inc 1 st at beg of rnd—37 sts.
Note: This extra st is the center underarm and is not included in the charted pattern. On any rnds that use A, knit with A. If rnd is worked without A, knit with whatever color is being used.

Next rnd: K1; work Chart A around rem 36 sts.

Next 2 rnds: Complete Chart A.

Next rnd: K1A; work Rnd 1 of Chart B around.

Next rnd (inc): K1A, M1, work Rnd 2 of Chart B to end, M1—39 sts.
Note: Work M1s using color that will maintain the pat, and work all inc'd sts on following rnd in expanded pat.

Continue working Chart B and M1 on each side of the center underarm st [every 2 rnds] 12 (11, 8, 2, 2) times, then [every 4 rnds] 2 (3, 6, 12, 12) times—67 sts.

Work even until sleeve measures approx 7 (7½, 8½, 10, 10½)"/18 (19, 21½, 25½, 26½)cm or ½"/1.25cm short of desired length.

Work 3-rnd Chart A.

Sleeve Facing

With C, work sleeve facing back and forth in reverse St st as follows:

Rows 1 and 3 (RS): Purl.

Rows 2 and 4: Knit.

BO loosely, with larger needle.

Finishing

Wet-block pieces.

Stabilize Steek Stitches

Set sewing machine to small sts. Place yoke under the machine foot and sew on column of sts adjacent to the center CC column of steek sts, beg at shoulder and ending at steek CO. Turn and sew back along column of sts on other side of CC column. It is important to sew into a column of sts and not in the "ladders" between the sts to make a much stronger steek. Sew at least 3 rows on each side of the CC sts.

Cut open armhole along CC line.

Rep for other armhole.

Right Shoulder Seam

Turn body inside out and transfer yoke sts to 2 circular needles. Join 20 (21, 22, 23, 24) right shoulder sts using 3-needle BO.

Transfer next 20 (21, 22, 23, 24) front and back sts to separate holders for neck; transfer rem 20 (21, 22, 23, 24) sts to separate holders for left shoulder.

Front Neckline

Mark a position 1½ (1¾, 2, 2¼, 2½)"/4 (4.5, 5, 5.5, 6.5) cm down from center front neck. Baste a curved line from this low point to the points where the shoulder sts meet the neck sts for front neck opening. Use sewing machine to sew along the marked front neck, sewing at least 3 rows with the machine.

Cut out neckline semicircle inside the machine stitching.

Buttonhole Band

Transfer back shoulder sts to needle.

Row 1 (RS): Join C; purl across.

Row 2: Work in k1, p1 rib across.

Schematics

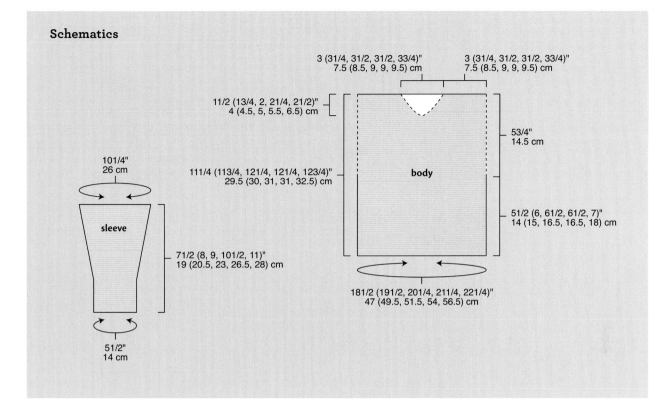

3 (31/4, 31/2, 31/2, 33/4)"
7.5 (8.5, 9, 9, 9.5) cm

3 (31/4, 31/2, 31/2, 33/4)"
7.5 (8.5, 9, 9, 9.5) cm

11/2 (13/4, 2, 21/4, 21/2)"
4 (4.5, 5, 5.5, 6.5) cm

53/4"
14.5 cm

101/4"
26 cm

111/4 (113/4, 121/4, 121/4, 123/4)"
29.5 (30, 31, 31, 32.5) cm

body

sleeve

51/2 (6, 61/2, 61/2, 7)"
14 (15, 16.5, 16.5, 18) cm

71/2 (8, 9, 101/2, 11)"
19 (20.5, 23, 26.5, 28) cm

181/2 (191/2, 201/4, 211/4, 221/4)"
47 (49.5, 51.5, 54, 56.5) cm

51/2"
14 cm

Buttonhole row: Maintain rib and work 3 [yo, k2tog] buttonholes evenly spaced along band.

Row 3: Work in established rib.

BO in rib.

Button Band Facing

Transfer front shoulder sts to needle.

Turning row 1 (RS): Join C; purl across.

Work 3 rows in St st.

Overlap button band with buttonhole band and tack in place at shoulder.

Join Sleeves

Sew sleeve into place along the line between steek sts and charted pat.

Sew facing to WS to cover the sewn steek edges.

Neck Edging

With RS facing and using C, pick up and knit approx 34 (35, 38, 40, 42) sts along front neck edge, knit across rem 20 (21, 22, 23, 24) back neck sts.

Row 1 (WS): Knit.

Rows 2–4: Work Chart A, back and forth.

Row 5 (turning row, WS): Knit.

Rows 7–8: Knit 1 row, purl 1 row, knit 1 row.

BO very loosely.

Sew facing to inside of neckline, folding along turning row.

Weave in all ends.

Block again.

Swedish Dubbelmössa

•••

This dubbelmössa (double hat) is the perfect place to pull a fisk ("fish") out of a mössa ("hat")! The hat is knit in two layers, making it reversible, so fish will come out of either end!The double layer, all-over pattern is based on the Binge knitting tradition of Halland, a province along the southwestern coast of Sweden. (*Binge* is pronounced "binga," derived from an old Swedish word for "knitting.")
The three-color pattern of this hat reflects traditional Binge colors—red, navy blue, and white—but here the traditional red with a brighter blue and creamy white better suits this lighthearted child's garment. A contemporary fish image stands out as a central design element alongside traditional Binge patterns. Knit this hat in wool for cold weather ice-fishing adventures or in cotton yarn for more temperate weather.

Design by W. J. Johnson, Saga Hill Designs

Sizes
0–3 (3–6, 6–12, 12–36) months

Finished Measurements
Circumference: 13½ (15, 16½, 18½)"/
34.5 (38, 42, 47)cm
Length: 7.5 (9, 10.5, 12)"/19 (23, 27, 30.5)cm

Materials
3 Cascade Yarns 220 Superwash Sport (heavy sport weight; 100% superwash merino wool; 136 yds/125m per 1¾/50g per skein): 1 (1, 1, 2) skein(s) each Sunset Orange #808 (A), Denim #845 (B) and Aran #817 (C)

Alternative cotton yarn: Cascade Yarns *Ultra Pima* (heavy sport weight; 100% pima cotton; 220 yds/209m per 3½ oz/100g skein): 1 skein each Lipstick Red #3755 (A), Indigo Blue #3793 (B) and Natural #3718 (C)

Size 3 (3.25mm) double-pointed and 16"/40.5cm circular needles or size needed to obtain gauge

Size E/4 (3.5mm) crochet hook

Stitch markers

Tapestry needle

Waste yarn (for provisional cast-on)

Gauge
24 sts and 28 rnds = 4"/10cm in stranded 2-color St st.
Adjust needle size as necessary to obtain correct gauge.

Special Technique

Crocheted provisional cast-on:
Using smooth waste yarn, crochet a chain about 5-10 sts more than desired cast-on st count. Using the project yarn, pick up loops through the purl-like bumps on the back of the chain. After working the first hat layer, you will remove the crochet chain to free the provisional CO sts to knit the second hat layer.

Pattern Notes

The hat is worked in-the-round, from the bottom up, beginning with the brim. After the first hat layer is complete, the provisional cast-on is unzipped and the new live stitches are put on the needle. The second layer is worked following the instructions for the first layer but using the other color chart.

Because the hat has two layers, the wrong side of the fabric will never be visible. It is not critical to weave in yarns not in use over wide areas because the strands won't be seen or caught on clothing.

When working the color pattern, cut yarns between pattern repeats as needed. Weave in these ends when first layer is finished. For second layer, weave in these ends before decreasing for the crown.

••• Instructions

First Layer

Body

Using provisional method and A, CO 92 (102, 112, 122) sts; pm for beg of rnd and join, taking care not to twist sts.

Knit 1 rnd, purl 1 rnd, knit 4 rnds.

Dec rnd: K8 (8, 8, 10), k2tog, [k13 (15, 17, 18), k2tog] 5 times, k7 (7, 7, 10)—86 (96, 106, 116) sts.

Knit 4 rnds.

Dec rnd: K7 (7, 7, 10), k2tog, [k12 (14, 16, 17), k2tog] 5 times, k7 (7, 7, 9)—80 (90, 100, 110) sts.

Knit 1 rnd, purl 1 rnd, knit 3 rnds.

Beg working color pat following Chart A; work Rnds 1–20 once, then rep [Rnds 12-20] 0 (1, 2, 3) times.

Sizes 0–3 (6–12) months only

Work Rnd 21 of chart.

Sizes 3–6 (12–36) months only

Dec rnd: Work Rnd 21 of chart and dec as follows: K22 (9), k2tog, [k43 (16), k2tog] 1 (5) times, k21 (9)—88 (104) sts.

Shape Crown—all sizes

Distribute sts evenly on 4 dpns with 20 (22, 25, 26) sts on each needle.

Work Rnd 22 of chart.

Dec rnd: Working Rnd 23 of chart, [work to last 2 sts on dpn, k2tog] 4 times around—19 (21, 24, 25) sts on each dpn.

Next 3 rnds: Maintaining established pat, work Rnds 24–26 of chart and dec 1 st at end of each dpn—16 (18, 21, 22) sts on each dpn.

Rep last 4 rnds until 8 sts rem (2 sts on each dpn).

Cut the yarns, leaving 18"/45cm tails. Thread the yarn last worked through the rem sts and pull tight; thread the other yarn through the center of the closed hole to the RS.

Make a crocheted tassel.

Chart A

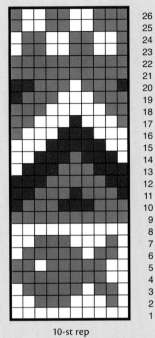

26
25
24
23
22
21
20
19
18
17
16
15
14
13
12
11
10
9
8
7
6
5
4
3
2
1

10-st rep

Chart B

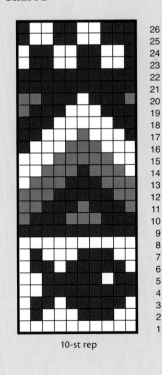

26
25
24
23
22
21
20
19
18
17
16
15
14
13
12
11
10
9
8
7
6
5
4
3
2
1

10-st rep

Color Key

■	A
■	B
□	C

Tassel

Holding the 2 tails together, crochet a chain about 2"/5cm long. Fasten off, but do not trim yarns yet.

Cut a piece of cardboard 2"/5cm wide. Cut one strand each of the colors used in the crochet chain, about 50"/127cm long. Holding the strands together, wrap the the yarns around the cardboard 10 times, then cut the yarns even at the bottom of the last wrap. Use the tail of the crochet chain to tie a knot around the top of the wrapped yarns to secure them. Cut the bottom of the tassel wraps to open them. Cut a 10"/25cm strand of A and wrap it tightly 5–6 times around the top of the tassel about ½"/ (1.25cm) below the top knot. Use a tapestry needle to whipstitch this wrap, tucking and weaving in the ends. Trim tassel ends.

Note: *If the tassel is shorter than the length of the crown decrease section, it shouldn't touch the baby's head on the inside layer, since the crown is meant to hang away from the head. Adjust tassel length as necessary. If it still seems too long, you can knot the crochet chain a few times next to where it emerges from the hat to shorten it.*

Second Layer

Unzip the provisional cast-on chain and transfer the live sts to needles.

Work 2nd layer as for first using B (instead of A) as the main color and following Chart B. End with a tassel wrapped with B. Remember to weave in ends of second layer pattern before decreasing for crown.

This hat is an example of Binge knitting. Binge became a knitting business through the key efforts of Berta Borgström (a prominent doctor's wife) and some others in the Halland province of Sweden. Their Halland Knitting Cooperative was founded in 1907 as winter work to support the troubled local economy. (Similar to the reasons that the Bohus Stickning organization was begun in the neighboring province of Bohuslan in the 1930s.)

KNITS OF THE
United Kingdom and Europe

Fair Isle Sweater

•••

Aran Sweater

•••

Sanquhar Bonnet

•••

Baby Beret and
Booties

•••

Spanish Lace Blanket

Fair Isle Sweater

•••

This little Fair Isle design has just enough patterning to make the knitting interesting and not too time-consuming. It's perfect as your first stranded knitting project.

Design by Melissa Leapman

Sizes
6 (12, 18) months

Finished Measurements
Chest circumference: 21 (24, 27)"/53.5 (61, 68.5)cm
Length: 11 (12, 13)"/28 (30.5, 33)cm

Materials

[2] Cascade 220 *Superwash Sport* (sport weight; 100% superwash merino wool; 136 yds/124m per 1¾ oz/ 50g skein): 3 skeins Periwinkle #844 (A), 1 skein each Green Apple #802 (B), Purple Hyacinth #1986 (C), Royal Purple #803 (D), and Lemon #820 (E)

Size 3 (3.25mm) needles

Size 5 (3.75mm) needles or size needed to obtain gauge

Stitch holders

Stitch markers

4 [½"/1.25cm] buttons
(JHB International's #70165 was used on sample garment)

Gauge
24 sts and 32 rows = 4"/10cm in 2-color St st with larger needles.

Adjust needle size as necessary to obtain correct gauge.

Pattern Stitches

1×1 Rib (odd number of sts)

Row 1 (RS): K1, *p1, k1; rep from * to end.

Row 2: P1, *k1, p1; rep from * to end.

Rep Rows 1 and 2 for pat.

Fair Isle Chart

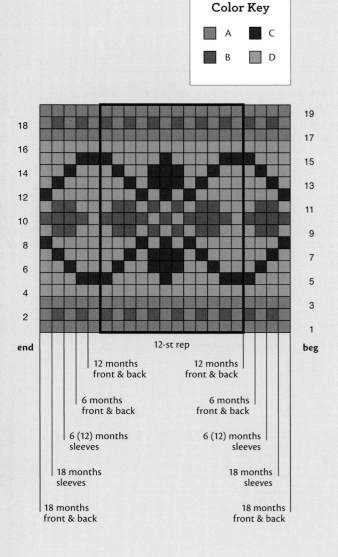

Color Key

A C

B D

••• Instructions

Back

With smaller needles and A, CO 63 (73, 81) sts.

Work in 1×1 Rib for 1"/2.5cm, ending with a WS row.

Change to larger needles; beg and end where indicated for your size, work 19-row Fair Isle pat following chart. Cut all yarns.

With A, work even in St st until piece measures approx 11 (12, 13)"/28 (30.5, 33)cm, ending with a RS row.

Next row (WS): P20 (25, 26) sts and slip them onto a holder for button band; BO rem sts.

Front

Work same as for back until piece measures approximately 9½ (10½, 11½)"/24 (26.5, 29)cm, ending with a WS row.

Shape Neck

Next row (RS): K22 (27, 29); join 2nd ball of yarn and BO center 19 (19, 23) sts, knit to end of row.

Working both sides at once with separate balls of yarn, dec 1 st each neck edge every row 2 (2, 3) times—20 (25, 26) sts rem each side.

Work even, if necessary, until piece measures 10½ (11¼, 12¼)"/26.5 (28.5, 31)cm, ending with a WS row.

Next row (RS): Slip first 20 (25, 26) sts to holder for buttonhole band; knit to end of row.

Work even on rem side until it measures same as back.

BO.

Sleeves

With smaller needles and A, CO 41 (41, 43) sts.

Work in 1x1 Rib for 1"/2.5cm, ending with a WS row.

Change to larger needles; work 19-row Fair Isle pat, then continue with A only.

At the same time, inc 1 st each side [every 4 rows] 6 (8, 6) times, then [every 6 rows] 2 (2, 4) times, working new sts into pat as they accumulate—57 (61, 63) sts.

Work even until piece measures approx 6½ (7½, 8½)"/16.5 (19, 21.5)cm.

BO.

Finishing

Block pieces to finished measurements.

Sew right shoulder seam.

Neckband

With RS facing, using smaller needles and A, pick up and knit 56 (56, 60) sts along neckline.

Row 1 (WS): *K1, p1; rep from * across.

Work 8 rows in established rib.

BO in rib.

Button band

With RS of back facing, using smaller needles and A, pick up and knit 6 sts along side of neckband, then k20 (25, 26) buttonband sts from holder—26 (31, 32) sts.

Work 6 rows in k1, p1 rib.

BO in rib

Place markers for 4 evenly-spaced buttons on band, with the first and last .25"/.5cm from side edges.

Buttonhole Band

Transfer 20 (25, 26) buttonhole band sts to smaller needle.

With RS facing, smaller needles, and A, work 1×1 Rib across sts, then pick up and knit 6 sts along neckband—26 (31, 32) sts.

Work 1 row in established rib.

Buttonhole row (RS): Cont in rib and make buttonholes opposite each marker on buttonband by working (k2tog, yo).

Work 6 rows even.

BO in rib.

With buttonhole band overlapping button band, sew top of armhole closed.

Place markers 4¾ (5, 5¼)"/12 (12.5, 13.5)cm down from shoulders.

Sew on sleeves between markers.

Sew sleeve and side seams.

Sew on buttons.

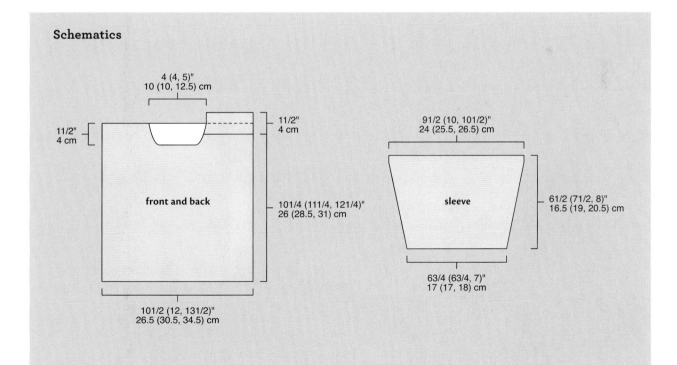

Schematics

4 (4, 5)"
10 (10, 12.5) cm

11/2"
4 cm

11/2"
4 cm

front and back

101/4 (111/4, 121/4)"
26 (28.5, 31) cm

101/2 (12, 131/2)"
26.5 (30.5, 34.5) cm

91/2 (10, 101/2)"
24 (25.5, 26.5) cm

sleeve

61/2 (71/2, 8)"
16.5 (19, 20.5) cm

63/4 (63/4, 7)"
17 (17, 18) cm

Aran Sweater

•••

This pullover has all the elements of a traditional Aran design in a pint-size piece.
Shaping is minimal so you can relax and enjoy knitting the textures.

Design by Melissa Leapman

Sizes
6 (12, 18) months

Finished Measurements
Chest: 20½ (24, 26½)"/52 (61, 67.5)cm
Length: 11 (12, 13)"/28 (30.5, 33)cm

Materials
 Lion Brand Yarns *Baby Wool* (worsted
weight; 100% easy-care wool;
98 yds/90m per 1.75 oz/50g ball): 4 (5, 5)
balls Almond #099

Size 6 (4mm) needles

Size 8 (5mm) needles or size needed to
obtain gauge

Cable needle

Stitch holders

4 [½"/1.25cm] buttons (JHB International's
#70165 was used on sample garment)

Gauge
18 sts and 24 rows = 4"/10cm in Double
Seed St with larger needles.
*Adjust needle size as necessary to obtain
correct gauge.*

Special Abbreviations

2 over 2 Left Cross (2/2 LC): Slip 2 sts to cn and hold in front, k2, k2 from cn.

2 over 2 Right Cross (2/2 RC): Slip 2 sts to cn and hold in back, k2, k2 from cn.

2 over 2 Left Purl Cross (2/2 LPC): Slip 2 sts to cn and hold in front, p2, k2 from cn.

2 over 2 Right Purl Cross (2/2 RPC): Slip 2 sts to cn and hold in back, k2, p2 from cn.

Pattern Stitches

1x1 Rib (even number of sts)

Row 1 (RS): *K1, p1; rep from * to end.

Rep Row 1 for pat.

Seed Stitch (odd number of sts)

Row 1 (RS): K1, *p1, k1; rep from * to end.

Rows 2 and 3: P1, *k1, p1; rep from * to end.

Row 4: Rep Row 1.

Rep Rows 1–4 for pat.

Cable Panel A (12-st panel)

Row 1 (RS): P1, k1-tbl, p1, 2/2 RC, k2, p1, k1-tbl, p1.

Row 2: K1, p1-tbl, k1, p6, k1, p1-tbl, k1.

Row 3: P1, k1-tbl, p1, k2, 2/2 LC, p1, k1-tbl, p1.

Row 4: Rep Row 2.

Rep Rows 1–4 for pat.

Cable Panel B (26-st panel)

Row 1 (RS): P3, [2/2 RC, p4] twice, 2/2 RC, p3.

Row 2: K3, p4, [k4, p4] twice, k3.

Row 3: P1, [2/2 RPC, 2/2 LPC] 3 times, p1.

Row 4: K1, p2, [k4, p4] twice, k4, p2, k1.

Row 5: P1, k2, p4, [2/2 LC, p4] twice, k2, p1.

Row 6: Rep Row 4.

Row 7: P1, [2/2 LPC, 2/2 RPC] 3 times, p1.

Row 8: Rep Row 2.

Rep Rows 1–8 for pat.

Stitch Key

- ☐ k on RS, p on WS
- ⊟ p on RS, k on WS
- ⊠ k1-tbl on RS, p1-tbl on WS
- 2/2 RC
- 2/2 LC
- 2/2 RPC
- 2/2 LPC

Cable Panel A

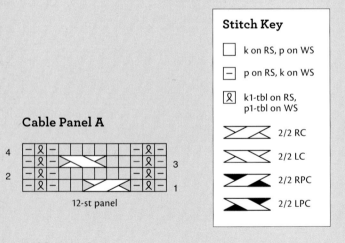

12-st panel

Cable Panel B

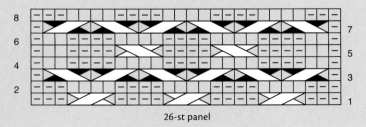

26-st panel

••• Instructions

Back

With smaller needles, CO 70 (78, 86) sts.

Work in 1×1 Rib for 1"/2.5cm, ending with a WS row.

Set-up row (RS): Change to larger needles; working Row 1 of each pattern, work Double Seed St across first 5 (9, 13) sts, pm, work Cable Panel A across next 12 sts, pm, work Double Seed St across next 5 sts, pm, work Cable Panel B across next 26 sts, pm, work Double Seed St across next 5 sts, pm, work Cable Panel A across next 12 sts, pm, work Double Seed St across last 5 (9, 13) sts.

Work even in established pats until piece measures approx 11 (12, 13)"/28 (30.5, 33)cm, ending with a RS row.

Next row (WS): Work across 20 (24, 26) sts and slip them onto holder for button band; BO rem sts.

Front

Work same as back until piece measures approximately 9½ (10½, 11½)"/24 (26.5, 29)cm, ending with a WS row.

Shape Neck

Next row (RS): Work across first 22 (26, 30) sts; join 2nd ball of yarn and BO center 26 sts, work to end of row.

Next 2 rows: Working both sides at once with separate balls of yarn, dec 1 st at each neck edge— 20 (24, 28) sts rem each side.

Work even, if necessary, until piece measures 10¼ (11¼, 12¼)"/26 (28.5, 31)cm, ending with a WS row.

Next row (RS): Slip first 20 (24, 28) sts to holder for buttonhole band; work across rem sts.

Work even on this side until it measures same as back.

BO.

Sleeves

With smaller needles, CO 30 (30, 32) sts.

Work in 1×1 Rib for 1"/2.5cm, ending with a WS row, and on last row, inc 1 st at end of row—31 (31, 33) sts.

Change to larger needles and Double Seed St.

Inc 1 st each side [every 4 rows] 5 (8, 6) times, then [every 6 rows] 1 (0, 2) times, working new sts into pat as they accumulate—43 (47, 49) sts.

Work even until piece measures 6½ (7½, 8)"/16.5 (19, 20.5)cm.

BO.

Schematics

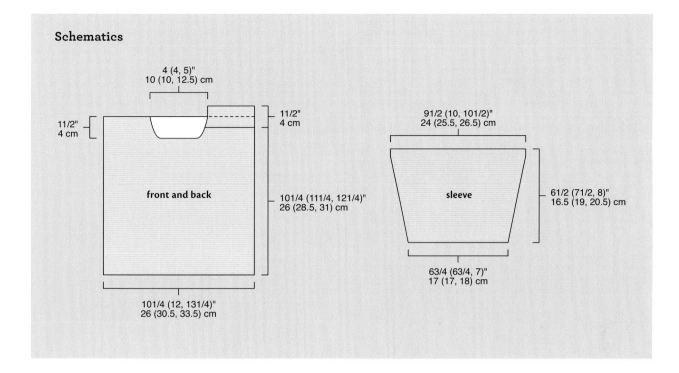

4 (4, 5)"
10 (10, 12.5) cm

11/2"
4 cm

11/2"
4 cm

front and back

101/4 (111/4, 121/4)"
26 (28.5, 31) cm

101/4 (12, 131/4)"
26 (30.5, 33.5) cm

91/2 (10, 101/2)"
24 (25.5, 26.5) cm

sleeve

61/2 (71/2, 8)"
16.5 (19, 20.5) cm

63/4 (63/4, 7)"
17 (17, 18) cm

Finishing

Block pieces to finished measurements.

Sew right shoulder seam.

Neckband

With RS facing and smaller needles, pick up and knit 56 (56, 60) sts along neckline.

Work in 1×1 Rib for 1"/2.5cm.

BO in rib.

Button band

With RS of back facing and smaller needles, pick up and knit 4 sts along side of neckband, work in 1×1 Rib across 20 (24, 28) button band sts from holder—24 (28, 32) sts.

Work 4 rows in 1×1 Rib.

BO in rib.

Place markers for 4 evenly-spaced buttons on band, with the first and last placed ¼"/.5cm from side edges.

Buttonhole Band

Transfer 20 (24, 28) sts from buttonhole band sts to smaller needle.

With RS facing and smaller needles, work 1×1 Rib across sts, then pick up and knit 4 along side of neckband—24 (28, 32) sts.

Work 1 WS row in 1×1 Rib.

Buttonhole row (RS): Cont in rib and make buttonholes opposite each marker on button band by working (k2tog, yo).

Work 2 rows even.

BO in rib.

With buttonhole band overlapping button band, sew top of armhole closed.

Place markers 4¾ (5, 5¼)"/12 (12.5, 13.5)cm down from shoulders.

Sew on sleeves between markers.

Sew sleeve and side seams.

Sew on buttons.

Sanquhar Bonnet

•••

This sophisticated bonnet marries the classic black-and-white Scottish
Sanquhar pattern with the chullu style cap of the Andes. Sanquhar,
an ancient town in the hills of southern Scotland, became well known by the
early nineteenth century for production of stockings, gloves, and other textiles.
Sanquhar gloves were prized for their ability to firmly hold horse reins in the
rain. The alternating pair of squares in this variation is known as Cornet & Drum.
It is distinctive of the Sanquhar family of patterns, which are anchored in
an 11-stitch grid or *dambrod*. As is historically done, you can create larger
sizing options by using a larger needle with the same yarn.

Design by Elanor Lynn

Sizes
3–12 months (1–2, 2–6+) years

Finished Measurements
Circumference: 15 (17, 19)"/38 (43, 48)cm

Materials
Cascade Yarns *Heritage* (fingering
weight; 75% superwash merino
wool/25% nylon; 437 yds/400m per 3½ oz/
100g skein): 1 skein each Black #5601 (A)
and Snow #5618 (B).

Size 1 (2.25mm) double-pointed needles or
size needed to obtain gauge

Stitch markers, 1 in contrast color for beg
of rnd

Tapestry needle

Gauge
47 sts and 52 rows = 4"/10cm] 2-color
stranded St st.
*Adjust needle size as necessary to obtain
correct gauge.*

••• Instructions

Border

Using provisional method of choice and A, CO 175 (195, 220) sts; distribute evenly on dpns, mark beg of rnds, and join.

Rnds 1–10: Work 2 reps of 5-rnd Border Chart.

Body

Rnd 1: Begin Body Chart, starting on Rnd 1 (12, 1) and inc 1 (3, 0) sts evenly around—176 (198, 220) sts.

Work 22 (33, 44) rnds even following Body Chart, ending with Rnd 1.

Crown

Set-up rnd: Working chart Rnd 2, [k11, pm] 16 (18, 20) times around.

Dec rnd: Maintaining established color pat, *knit to 2 sts before marker, k2tog, slip marker; rep from * around—160 (180, 200) sts.

Maintaining charted pattern with black spines "eating" into patterned squares, rep Dec rnd [every 4 rnds] 9 more times; cut B when it is no longer being used—16 (18, 20) sts.

With A, knit 3 rnds.

Last rnd: K2tog around—8 (9, 10) sts.

Cut A, leaving a 6"/15cm tail.

Using tapestry needle, thread tail through rem sts, and pull tight.

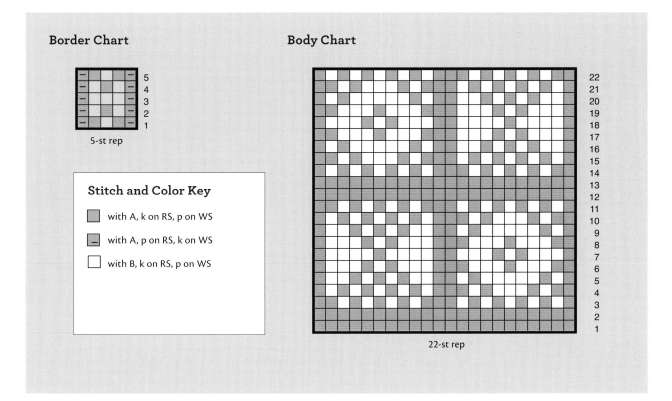

Border Chart

5-st rep

Body Chart

22-st rep

Stitch and Color Key

- with A, k on RS, p on WS
- with A, p on RS, k on WS
- with B, k on RS, p on WS

Stitch and Color Key

- ⬜ with A, k on RS, p on WS
- ⬜ with A, k on WS
- ⬜ with A, ssk on RS, ssp on WS
- ⬜ with A, k2tog on RS, p2tog on WS
- ⬜ with B, k on RS, p on WS

Flap Chart

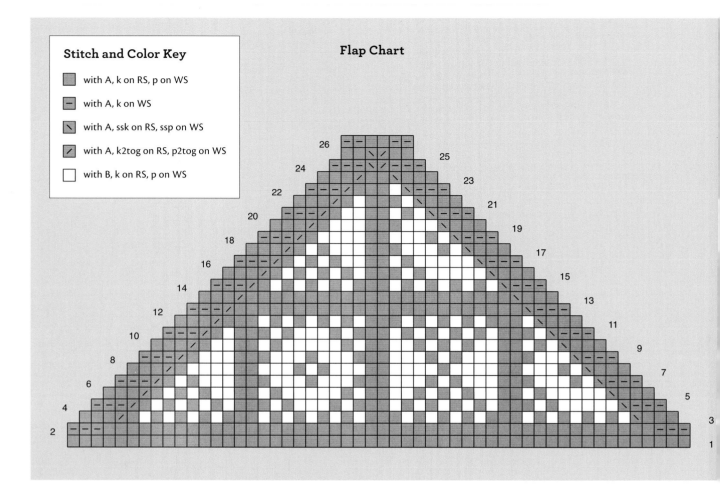

Flaps

Release sts from provisional CO and distribute on dpns.

Right Flap and Tie

Join A; BO 36 (47, 58) sts.

Work Rows 1–24 of Flap Chart—6 sts.

With A, rep [Rows 25 and 26] 18 times or to desired length.

Next row (RS): K1, k2tog, ssk, k1—4 sts.

Next row: Ssp, p2tog—2 sts.

Next row: K2tog—1 st.

Cut yarn and fasten off last st.

Left Flap and Tie

Join A adjacent to Right Flap; BO 36 (47, 58) sts.

Complete left flap and tie as for right.

Tassels (Make 2)

With A and B held together, wrap yarns 21 times around the short side of a standard business card. Cut yarns, leaving a 12"/30.5cm tail. Draw tail through top of loops. Slide loops off card onto a pencil. Wrap tail around tassel under the pencil to create tassel top. Secure tail end. Cut through bottom of loops and attach tassel to end of tie.

Finishing

Weave in ends.

Block as desired.

Baby Beret and Booties

Here's the perfect ensemble for an outing to the Eiffel Tower. The French baby beret and booties use a delicate eyelet lace pattern on the bands. On the beret, the bands of lace extend over the top of the hat and merge together to form an I-cord tip. The lace band on the booties extends down the front of the foot, and the holes in the lace pattern could be used for threading ribbon in a shoelace-like pattern.

Design by Sue Flanders

Finished Measurements
Beret
Circumference: 14"/34cm

Booties
Height: 2"/5cm
Length: 3½"/8.5cm

Materials

Knit Picks *Swish DK* (DK weight; 100% superwash merino wool; 123 yds/112m per 1¾ oz/50g skein): 1 skein White or Carnation

Size 4 (3.5mm) double-pointed needles or size needed to obtain gauge

Stitch markers

Waste yarn or stitch holders

Tapestry needle

Gauge
24 sts and 28 rnds = 4"/10cm in St st.
Adjust needle size as necessary to obtain correct gauge.

Pattern Note

The Eyelet Rib pattern is 4 rounds. Each repeat increases by 1 stitch on Rnd 2 and decreases by 1 stitch on Rnd 4. After the border rib is complete, the hat is divided into 5 sections, with 8 stitches being continued in Eyelet Rib alternating with stockinette stitch sections that are first increased to shape the sides, then decreased to form the crown. When counting the Eyelet Rib stitches during shaping, always count each section as 8 stitches.

Special Abbreviations

Centered Double Decrease (CDD): Slip 2 sts as if to k2tog, k1, pass the slipped sts over.

Make 1 Left (M1L): Insert LH needle from front to back under the running thread between the last st worked and next st on LH. With RH needle, knit into the back of this loop.

Make 1 Right (M1R): Insert LH needle from back to front under the running thread between the last st worked and next st on LH needle. With RH needle, knit into the front of this loop.

Slip marker (sm): Slip marker from LH needle to RH needle.

••• Beret Instructions

CO 75 sts; distribute sts on dpns, mark beg of rnd and join, taking care not to twist sts.

Work 4 rnds in Eyelet Rib as follows:

Eyelet Rib (multiple of 5 sts, inc to 6 sts)
Rnd 1: *P1, k1, p1, k2; rep from * around.

Rnd 2: *P1, k1, p1, *k1, yo, k1; rep from * around—6-st rep.

Rnd 3: *P1, k1, p1, k3; rep from * around.

Rnd 4: *P1, k1, p1, k3, pass 3rd st on RH needle over the 2 sts; rep from * around—5-st rep.

Increase Sides
Rnd 1: *Work 8 sts in established Eyelet Rib, pm, k7, pm; rep from * 4 times.

Rnd 2: *Work Eyelet Rib to marker, sm, M1L, knit to next marker, M1R, sm; rep from * around—10 sts inc'd.

Rep [Rnds 1 and 2] 3 more times—115 sts.

Work 8 rnds in established pat.

Decrease Sides
Rnd 1: *Work Eyelet Rib to marker, sm, ssk, knit to 2 sts before next marker, k2tog, sm; rep from * around—10 sts dec'd.

Rnd 2: *Work Eyelet Rib to marker, sm, knit to next marker, sm; rep from * around.

Rep [Rnds 1 and 2] 5 more times—55 sts rem.

Crown
Rnd 1: *Work Eyelet Rib to marker, sm, k1, k2tog, pass 2nd st on RH needle over the first st, sm; rep from * around—45 sts.

Rnd 2: *Work Eyelet Rib to marker, sm, p1, sm; rep from * around.

Rnd 3: *Work Eyelet Rib to 1 st before marker p1, (remove marker, slip next st on LH needle to RH needle, then remove next marker), slip st back to LH needle then p2tog, pass 2nd st on RH needle over first st; rep from * around, moving beg of rnd marker—35 sts.

Rnd 4: Work even.

Rnd 5: Work 5 sts, *k1, k2tog, pass 2nd st on RH needle over first st, work 4 sts in Lace pat; rep from * 3 times, k1, k2tog, pass 2nd st on RH needle over first st, moving beg of rnd marker—25 sts.

Rnd 6: Work even.

Rnd 7: *Work 3 sts, *p1, p2tog, pass 2nd st over first, work 2 sts; rep from * 3 times, p2, p2tog, pass 2nd st over first, moving beg of rnd marker—15 sts.

Rnd 8: Work even . K2tog around until 5 sts rem.

Place all 5 sts on 1 dpn and work 5 I-cord rnds as follows: *K5, do not turn; slip sts to other end of dpn, pull yarn around back; rep from *.

Cut yarn, leaving a 6"/15cm tail. Thread tail through rem sts, pull tight, then secure tail.

••• Bootie Instructions

Cuff

CO 30 sts, pm for beg of rnd and join, taking care not to twist sts.

Work 9 rnds in Eyelet Rib.

Top Flap

Row 1 (RS): K6 and place on holder, work next 11 sts in est Eyelet Rib, *(Note: This is Row 2 of Eyelet Rib, so these 11 sts increased to 13 sts)*, place rem 13 sts on holder.

Top flap is worked back and forth in Eyelet Rib on these sts as follows:

Row 2 (WS): P1, [k1, p3, k1, p1] twice.

Row 3: K1, [p1, k3, pass 3rd st on RH needle over, p1, k1] twice.

Row 4: P1, [k1, p2, k1, p1] twice.

Row 5: K1, [p1, k1, yo, k1, p1, k1, p1, k1, yo, k1] twice, p1, k1.

Rows 6–16: Rep [Rows 2–5] twice, then work Rows 2–4.

Row 17: Ssk, k1, yo, k1, p1, k1, p1, k1, yo, k1, k2tog—2 sts dec'd.

Row 18: P4, k1, p1, k1, p4.

Row 19: Ssk, k2, pass 3rd st on RH needle over the 2 sts, p1, k1, p1, k2, k2tog, pass 3rd st on RH needle over the 2 sts, do not turn—7 sts.

Sides

Transfer 19 sts on hold to dpns.

With RS facing, pick up and knit 8 sts along side of flap, k9, pm, k10, pick up and knit 8 sts along opposite side of flap, knit around to marker—42 sts.

Knit 6 rnds.

Purl 1 rnd.

Sole

Rnd 1: K3, CDD, k10, CDD, k5, CDD, k10, CDD, k2—34 sts.

Rnd 2 and 4: Knit.

Rnd 3: K2, CDD, k8, CDD, k3, CDD, k8, CDD, k1—26 sts.

Rnd 5: K1, CDD, k6, CDD, k1, CDD, k6, CDD—18 sts.

Transfer sts so that 9 sts are on 1 dpn and 9 are on other, with bottom of sole in center.

Graft sole closed using Kitchener st.

Spanish Lace Blanket

•••

Some of the earliest lace knitting pattern stitches come from Spain, where knitting was done in the round and there were no plain rows between the lace rows. Although this blanket is knit back and forth, the ornate, delicate lace hints at the mantillas worn by Spanish dancers. This heirloom blanket is meant to be a special gift for a first grandchild, a long-awaited addition to the family, or perhaps for a best friend's new little one. This project is perfect for the experienced lace knitter.

Design by Donna Druchunas

Size
Approx 28 x 24"/71 x 61cm, blocked

Materials
 Knit Picks *Swish Worsted* (worsted weight; 100% superwash merino wool; 110 yds/100m per 1.75 oz/50g ball): 7 balls Sugar Plum

Size 7 (4.5mm) circular needle at least 32"/80cm long or size needed to obtain gauge

Spare knitting needle

9 stitch markers, 1 in contrasting color

Tapestry needle

Gauge
20 sts and 28 rows = 4"/10cm in St st.
Adjust needle size as necessary to obtain correct gauge.

Special Abbreviation

Centered Double Dec (CDD): Slip next 2 sts as if to k2tog, k1, pass slipped sts over.

Special Technique

3-needle bind-off: With RS tog and needles parallel, using a 3rd needle, knit tog a st from the front needle with 1 from the back. *Knit tog a st from the front and back needles, and slip the first st over the 2nd to bind off. Rep from * across, then fasten off last st.

Pattern Notes

Blanket is made in two halves that are joined in the center with 3 needle bind-off.

Lace Chart has yarnovers and decreases on every row. Pay careful attention while knitting.

Pattern Stitch

Lace Pattern (multiple of 33 sts)

Row 1 (WS): K2, [ssp, yo, p2] 3 times, k2, yo, p4, p2tog, p5, ssp, p4, yo.

Row 2 (RS): K1, yo, k4, ssk, k3, k2tog, k4, yo, k1, p2, [k2tog, yo, k2] 3 times, p2.

Row 3: K2, [ssp, yo, p2] 3 times, k2, p2, yo, p4, p2tog, p1, ssp, p4, yo, p2.

Row 4: K3, yo, k4, CDD, k4, yo, k3, p2, [k2tog, yo, k2] 3 times, p2.

Rows 5–12: Rep Rows 1–4 twice.

Row 13: Yo, p4, p2tog, p5, ssp, p4, yo, k2, [ssp, yo, p2] 3 times, k2.

Row 14: P2, [k2tog, yo, k2] 3 times, p2, k1, yo, k4, ssk, k3, k2tog, k4, yo, k1.

Row 15: P2, yo, p4, p2tog, p1, ssp, p4, yo, p2, k2, [ssp, yo, p2] 3 times, k2.

Row 16: P2, [k2tog, yo, k2] 3 times, p2, k3, yo, k4, CDD, k4, yo, k3.

Rows 17–24: Rep Rows 13–16 twice.

Lace Chart

Stitch Key

- ☐ k on RS, p on WS
- ☐ p on RS, k on WS
- ☐ yo
- ☐ ssk on RS, ssp on WS
- ☐ k2tog on RS, p2tog on WS
- ☐ CDD
- ☐ 4-row rep

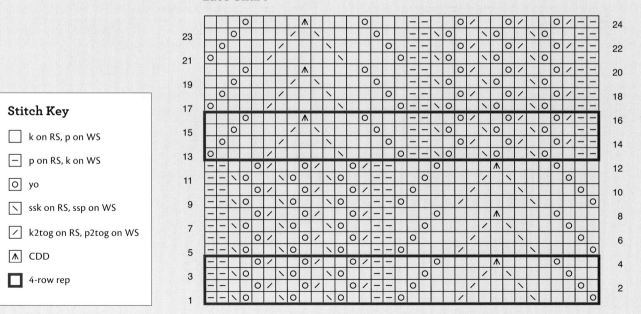

••• Instructions

Blanket (Make 2 pieces alike)

CO 140 sts.

Knit 8 rows.

Set-up row (WS): K4, pm, [work Lace pat across next 33 sts, pm] 4 times, k4.

Continuing to knit the first and last 4 sts of every row, complete the 24-row Lace pat.

Purl 1 row.

Do not BO.

Make 2nd half.

With RS together, join using 3-needle BO.

Border

With RS facing and beg at center seam, *pick up and knit 1 st in each garter ridge to corner, pm, pick up 1 st in corner, pm, pick up and knit 1 st for each st to corner, pm, pick up 1 st in corner; rep from * once, pick up and knit 1 st in each garter ridge to seam, place CC marker to indicate beg of rnd and join.

Note: Exact number of stitches does not matter.

Work in the round as follows:

Rnd 1: *Knit to marker, sm, yo, knit to next marker, yo, sm; rep from * 3 more times, knit to end of rnd—2 sts inc'd each corner.

Rnd 2: *Purl to marker, slip marker, knit to next marker, slip marker; rep from * 3 more times, purl to end of rnd.

Rep [Rnds 1 and 2] 7 more times.

Purl 1 rnd.

BO very loosely.

Finishing

Weave in ends. Wash and dry flat to block, stretching slightly and pinning to open the lace pattern if desired.

KNITS OF
the West

Andean Lace
Baby Chullo

•••

Andean Kitty or Bird Cap

•••

Blueberry
Forest Sweater

•••

Mittens for Sven

•••

Felted Baby Tote Set

Andean Lace Baby Chullo

• • •

The intricate colorwork hats worn by boys and men in Peru are quite famous,
but lace caps are less well known. The originals were knit with natural white yarn
at a very fine gauge on tiny needles; sometimes the knitters even used
bicycle spokes! Made in a soft pastel yarn, this adaptation is perfect for
modern comfort and faster knitting. The lace patterns are easy enough
for new lace knitters, making this a perfect skill-building project.

Design by Donna Druchunas

Size
3–6 months

Finished Measurements
Circumference: 15"/38cm

Materials

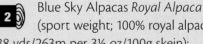 Blue Sky Alpacas *Royal Alpaca*
(sport weight; 100% royal alpaca;
288 yds/263m per 3½ oz/100g skein):
1 skein Seaglass #708

Size 3 (3.25mm) double-pointed needles
or size needed to obtain gauge

8 stitch markers, 1 in contrasting color for
beginning of round

Tapestry needle

Gauge
32 sts and 40 rnds = 4"/10cm in St st.
*Adjust needle size as necessary to obtain
correct gauge.*

Pattern Notes

Two earflaps are worked back and forth

Chart A

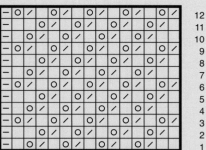

15-st rep

Chart B

15-st rep

Chart C

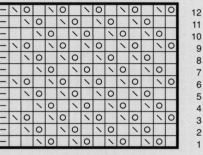

15-st rep

Pattern Stitches

Lace Pattern A (multiple of 15 sts)

Rnd 1: *[K1, yo, ssk] 4 times, k2, p1; rep from * around.

Rnd 2: *K2, [yo, ssk, k1] 4 times, p1; rep from * around.

Rnd 3: *[Yo, ssk, k1] 4 times, yo, ssk, p1; rep from * around.

Rnd 4: *[K1, yo, ssk] 4 times, k2, p1; rep from * around.

Rnd 5: *K2, [yo, ssk, k1] 4 times, p1; rep from * around.

Rnd 6: *[Yo, ssk, k1] 4 times, yo, ssk, p1; rep from * around.

Rnd 7: *[K1, yo, ssk] 4 times, k2, p1; rep from * around.

Rnd 8: *K2, [yo, ssk, k1] 4 times, p1; rep from * around.

Rnd 9: *[Yo, ssk, k1] 4 times, yo, ssk, p1; rep from * around.

Rnd 10: *[K1, yo, ssk] 4 times, k2, p1; rep from * around.

Rnd 11: *K2, [yo, ssk, k1] 4 times, p1; rep from * around.

Rnd 12: *[Yo, ssk, k1] 4 times, yo, ssk, p1; rep from * around.

Lace Pattern B (multiple of 15 sts)

Rnd 1: *[K1, yo, ssk] 4 times, k2, p1; rep from * around.

Rnd 2: *K2, [yo, ssk, k1] 4 times, p1; rep from * around.

Rnd 3: *K3, [yo, ssk, k1] 3 times, yo, ssk, p1; rep from * around.

Rnd 4: *[K1, yo, ssk] 4 times, k2, p1; rep from * around.

Rnd 5: *K2, [yo, ssk, k1] 4 times, p1; rep from * around.

Rnd 6: *K3, [yo, ssk, k1] 3 times, yo, ssk, p1; rep from * around.

Rnd 7: *K3, [k2tog, yo, k1] 3 times, k2tog, yo, p1; rep from * around.

Rnd 8: *K2, [k2tog, yo, k1] 4 times, p1; rep from * around.

Rnd 9: *[K1, k2tog, yo] 4 times, k2, p1; rep from * around.

Rnd 10: *[K2tog, yo, k1] 3 times, k2tog, yo, k3, p1; rep from * around.

Rnd 11: *K2, [k2tog, yo, k1] 4 times, p1; rep from * around.

Rnd 12: *[K1, k2tog, yo] 4 times, k2, p1; rep from * around.

Rnd 13: *[K2tog, yo, k1] 3 times, k2tog, yo, k3, p1; rep from * around.

Lace Pattern C (multiple of 15 sts)

Rnd 1: *[K1,yo, ssk] 4 times, k2, p1; rep from * around.

Rnd 2: *K2, [yo, ssk, k1] 4 times, p1; rep from * around.

Rnd 3: *[Yo, ssk, k1] 4 times, yo, ssk, p1; rep from * around.

Rnd 4: *[K1,yo, ssk] 4 times, k2, p1; rep from * around.

Rnd 5: *K2, [yo, ssk, k1] 4 times, p1; rep from * around.

Rnd 6: *[Yo, ssk, k1] 4 times, yo, ssk, p1; rep from * around.

Rnd 7: *[K1,yo, ssk] 4 times, k2, p1; rep from * around.

Rnd 8: *K2, [yo, ssk, k1] 4 times, p1; rep from * around.

Rnd 9: *[Yo, ssk, k1] 4 times, yo, ssk, p1; rep from * around.

Rnd 10: *[K1,yo, ssk] 4 times, k2, p1; rep from * around.

Rnd 11: *K2, [yo, ssk, k1] 4 times, p1; rep from * around.

Rnd 12: *[Yo, ssk, k1] 4 times, yo, ssk, p1; rep from * around.

••• Instructions

Earflaps (Make 2)
CO 3 sts.

Row 1 (RS): Knit.

Rows 2 and 4 (WS): Purl.

Row 3: K1, M1, k1, M1, k1—5 sts.

Row 5: K1, M1, knit to last st, M1, k1—7 sts.

Row 6: Purl.

Rep [Rows 5 and 6] 7 times—21 sts.

Cut yarn and transfer sts to holder.

Rep for 2nd earflap, but leave sts on needle.

Body
CO 17 sts, knit across earflap sts, CO 44 sts (front of hat), knit across earflap sts from holder, CO 17 sts; pm for beg of rnd and center back of hat, then join, being careful not to twist sts—120 sts.

[Knit 1 rnd, purl 1 rnd] 3 times.

Work 12-rnd Lace Pattern A.

[Knit 1 rnd, purl 1 rnd] 3 times.

Work 13-rnd Lace Pattern B.

[Knit 1 rnd, purl 1 rnd] 3 times.

Work 12-rnd Lace Pattern C.

[Knit 1 rnd, purl 1 rnd] 3 times, and on last rnd, pm every 15 sts around.

Crown
Dec rnd: [Knit to 2 sts before marker, k2tog] 8 times around—112 sts.

Knit 13 rnds.

Rep Dec rnd—104 sts.

Knit 12 rnds even.

Rep Dec rnd—96 sts.

Knit 11 rnds.

Rep Dec rnd—88 sts.

Continue decreasing, working 1 rnd fewer between Dec rnds until 16 sts rem.

Cut yarn, leaving a 6"/15cm tail. Thread tail through rem sts, pull tight to gather, then secure tail to WS.

Finishing

Ties
With RS facing, pick up and knit 4 sts at bottom tip of earflap.

*Do not turn; slip sts to left needle; k4; rep from * until cord measures 15"/38cm or desired length. BO.

Rep on other ear flap.

Weave in ends. Wash cap. Dry flat to block, stretching slightly and pinning to open the lace pats if desired.

Andean Kitty or Bird Cap

• • •

These cute little caps are sure to please little ones while keeping their ears warm, too. Choose between the kitty motif or the bird motif—or make one of each! Even though the yarn used for this hat is wool, it's machine washable—and it's also easy for working color patterns.

Design by Nancy J. Thomas

Size
18–48 months

Finished Measurements
Circumference: 14½"/37cm (hat will stretch to fit head)
Length: 10"/25.5cm with cuff unfolded (8"/20.5cm with cuff folded)

Materials
Kitty cap:

3 Filatura Di Crosa *Zara* (DK weight; 100% superwash merino wool; 136 yds/125m per 1¾oz/50g ball): 1 ball each, Charcoal Heather #1468 (A), Maize #1913 (B), Rust #1921 (C), Navy Blue #1389 (D), and Red #1466 (E)

Bird cap:

3 Filatura Di Crosa *Zara* (DK weight; 100% superwash merino wool; 136 yds/125m per 1.75oz/50g ball): 1 ball each, Red #1466 (A), Charcoal Heather #1468 (B), Maize #1948 (C), Rust #1921 (D), and Blue #0430 (E)

Both styles:
Size 6 (4mm) double-pointed needles (set of 4) or size needed to obtain gauge

Tapestry needle

Gauge
22 sts and 24 rnds = 4"/10cm in 2-color stranded St st.
Adjust needle size as necessary to obtain correct gauge.

Pattern Notes

When working color pattern, weave in yarn not in use if carried more than 4 stitches.

The beginning of the round is at the back of the hat. If you are making the Kitty Cap, there will be 2 consecutive rust cats on blue background at back.

... Instructions

Hat

With A, CO 80 sts. Distribute sts over 3 dpns as follows: 28-24-28; mark beg of rnd and join, taking care not to twist sts.

Work 4 rnds in k2, p2 rib.

Continuing in established rib, work 2-rnd stripes in following color order: B, A, C, A, D, A, E. Cut all yarns but A. (For the bird cap, work 4-rnd stripes with 3 rnds of A in between.)

Continue with A only until ribbing measures about 5"/11.5cm.

Change to St st, continuing with A.

Next rnd: *K6, k2tog; rep from * 9 times more —70 sts.

Knit 5 rnds.

For Kitty Cap

Work 13-rnd Kitty Chart, working the 28-st rep twice, ending with the last 14 sts of chart.

Change to A; work even in St st until hat measures 8"/20.5cm.

Kitty Chart

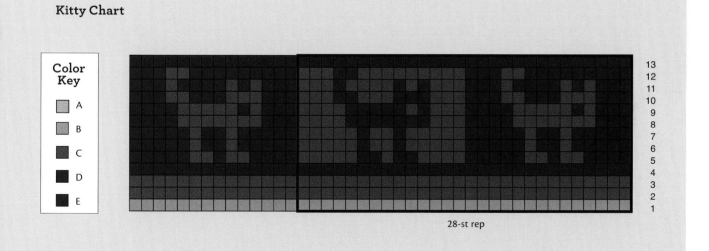

Color Key

- A
- B
- C
- D
- E

13
12
11
10
9
8
7
6
5
4
3
2
1

28-st rep

Yellow Bird Chart

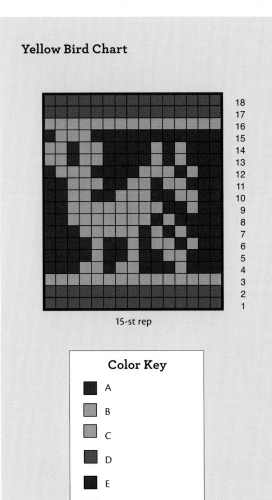

18
17
16
15
14
13
12
11
10
9
8
7
6
5
4
3
2
1

15-st rep

Color Key

■ A
■ B
■ C
■ D
■ E

■ knit with C,
French knots with E

For Bird Cap

Work 16-rnd Bird Chart 6 times.

Change to B; work 1 rnd.

Change to A; work 4 rnds.

Change to D.

Shape Crown

Rnd 1: [K2tog, k3] 14 times—56 sts.

Next 3 rnds: Knit.

Rnd 5: [K2tog, k2] 14 times—42 sts.

Next 3 rnds: Knit.

Rnd 9: [K2tog, k1] 14 times—28 sts.

Next 2 rnds: Knit.

Rnd 12: [K2tog] 14 times—14 sts.

Next rnd: Knit.

Rnd 14: [K2tog] 7 times—7 sts.

Rnd 15: [K2tog] 3 times, k1—4 sts.

Work 4-st I-cord with 2 dpns as follows: *K4, do not turn; slip sts to other end of dpn; pull yarn around back; rep from * until I-cord measures 2"/5cm.

Next row: K2tog twice, pass the first st on needle over the 2nd, then fasten off last st.

Tie I-cord in an overhand knot.

Weave in ends.

Block as desired.

Blueberry Forest Sweater

• • •

This toddler sweater was inspired by the landscape of the canoe country in the far northern part of Minnesota, where the mother and daughter designers go camping with their family. It's a place of paddling on lakes and camping on islands, cooking over fires and singing songs around them, hiking sunny hills and filling hats and water bottles with the small, delicious wild blueberries that grow among the wild roses and over the lichen-covered rocks. The trip that inspired this sweater took place just a year after a major forest fire had swept through the lake region. Already the shores were green, as the forest continued its slow growth, and the blueberries were particularly wonderful. The memories of that landscape provided the colors for this special design.

Design by Myra Arnold and Libby Johnson

Sizes

12 (24) months

Finished Measurements

Chest: 18 (20¾)"/46 (53)cm
Length: 11¾ (13¾)"/30 (35)cm

Materials

Size 12 months:

1 Rauma *Finullgarn* (fingering weight; 100% wool; 180 yds/165m per 1¾ oz/50g skein): 2 skeins Grass #430 (A), 1 skein each Navy #449 (B), Sky #451 (C), Chicory #472 (D), Arctic Blue #4406(E), Avocado #455 (F), and Cocoa #422 (G); about 5 yds/5m Lemon #4405 (H), and 2 yds/2m Red #418 (I)

Size 2 (2.75mm) 16"/40cm circular needle

Size 4 (3.5mm) 16"/40cm circular and double-pointed needles (set of 4) or size needed to obtain gauge

Size 24 months:

2 Cascade Yarns *220 Sport* (sport weight yarn; 100% Peruvian Highland wool; 164 yds/150m per 1¾ oz/50g skein): 2 skeins Highland Green #9430 (A); 1 each Navy #8393 (B), Colonial Blue Heather #9326 (C), West Point Blue Heather #9325 (D), Sage #9592 (E), Turtle #2452 (F), and Brown #8686 (G); about 5 yds/5m Goldenrod #7827 (H) and 2 yds/2m Ruby #9404 (I)

Size 4 (3.5mm) 16"/40cm circular needle

Size 6 (4mm) 16"/40cm circular and double-pointed needles (set of 4) or size needed to obtain gauge

Both sizes:

Stitch markers

Tapestry needle

Sewing machine

6 [½"/1.25cm] buttons

Gauge

Size 12 months: 30 sts and 31 rnds = 4"/10cm in stranded 2-color St st using larger needle

Size 24 months: 26 sts and 27 rnds = 4"/ 10 cm in stranded 2-color St st using larger needle.
Adjust needle size as necessary to obtain correct gauge.

Pattern Notes

The pattern text is the same for both sizes, except for sleeve length. The 12-month size uses fingering weight yarn; the 24-month size uses sport weight yarn.

The sweater is worked in the round from the bottom up. Sleeve and bottom edges are hemmed.

There are 6 stitch steeks between the fronts and at the armholes, each of which will be cut open later. Work the steek stitches as follows: If two colors are used in a patterning round, alternate the colors in the steek. Keep the edge stitches at the beginning and end of steek in the same color as long as you are carrying that color. Change colors for next pattern round in the middle of the front steek. There is no need to weave in ends, just leave a 4"/10cm or so end hanging. If you are going to use that same color again in a few rows, you can let it hang at the steek and pick it up again when needed. All these ends will be secured when you sew the steek with a zigzag stitch on the sewing machine. Steek stitches are not included in the stitch counts.

The charted patterns don't necessarily use complete repeats. This makes no difference in the appearance of the sweater.

••• Instructions

Body

With smaller needles and C, CO 135 sts.

Work 6 rows back and forth in St st.

Turning ridge (RS): Purl.

Begin working in the round and set up front steek as follows: Pm, cast on 6 steek sts, pm, knit to end of rnd.

Knit 5 rnds.

Change to larger needle.

Work Rnds 1–41 of Chart A.

Divide for Armholes

Next rnd: Working Rnd 42 of Chart A, k32 for right front, BO 3 for underarm, k65 for back, BO 3 for underarm, k32 for left front, ending at front steek.

Next rnd (add armhole steeks): Working Rnd 43 of Chart A, knit across right front, pm, CO 6 sts for right armhole steek, pm; knit across back, pm, CO 6 sts for left armhole steek, pm; knit across left front.

Complete Chart A, working the 3 steeks between the markers.

Next rnd: Work Chart B across right front, work Chart C across back, work Chart D across left front.

Continue until 26-rnd charts are complete.

Change to Chart E and work 2 rnds, ending before the front steek.

Chart A

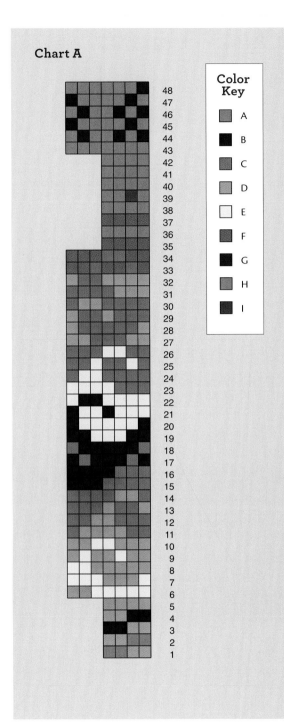

Color Key	
■	A
■	B
■	C
■	D
□	E
■	F
■	G
■	H
■	I

Neck Shaping

Next rnd: Continuing Chart E, BO 6 steek sts; BO 4 right front sts, work in established pat to end, turn.

Begin working back and forth in rows, completing Chart E, and shape neck as follows:

BO 4 sts at beg of next row, then BO 3 sts at beg of next 3 rows.

Next row (WS): BO 3 sts, work across rem left front sts, work across steek, work 26 back sts, BO 13 sts for back neck, work to end of row—22 front sts and 26 back sts rem each side.

Transfer left front and left back shoulder sts to holder; continue working on right front and back sts only.

Right Front/Back Neck Shaping

Row 1 (RS): Ssk, work to end of row—21 front sts.

Row 2: BO 3, work to end of row—23 back sts.

Row 3: Work even.

Row 4: BO 2 sts, work to end—21 back sts.

Row 5: Work to marker, BO 6 steek sts, work to end.

With WS facing, join front and back shoulders using 3-needle BO.

Left Front/Back Neck Shaping

Transfer Left Front and Back sts to needle; with RS facing, rejoin yarn at back neck edge.

Row 1 (RS): BO3, work to end of row—23 back sts.

Row 2: P2tog, work to end of row—21 front sts.

Row 3: BO 2 sts, work to end—21 back sts.

Row 4: Work even.

Row 5: Work to marker, BO 6 steek sts, work to end.

With WS facing, join front and back shoulders using 3-needle BO.

Chart B (Right Front)

26
25
24
23
22
21
20
19
18
17
16
15
14
13
12
11
10
9
8
7
6
5
4
3
2
1

Color Key

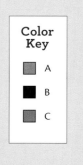

A

B

C

Chart C (Back)

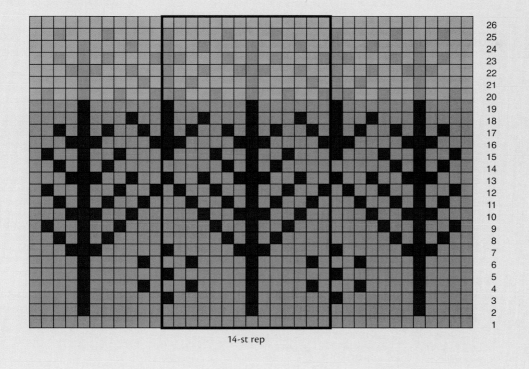

26
25
24
23
22
21
20
19
18
17
16
15
14
13
12
11
10
9
8
7
6
5
4
3
2
1

14-st rep

Chart D (Left Front)

26
25
24
23
22
21
20
19
18
17
16
15
14
13
12
11
10
9
8
7
6
5
4
3
2
1

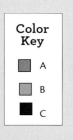

Color Key

A
B
C

Neck Band

With RS facing and using smaller circular needle and E, pick up and knit 20 sts along right front neck, 38 sts along back neck, and 20 sts along left front neck—78 sts.

Row 1 (WS): P2, *k2, p2; rep from * to end.

Row 2: K2, *p2, k2; rep from * to end.

Rep Rows 1 and 2 twice more.

BO loosely in rib.

Cut Steeks

With smooth, brightly colored waste yarn, baste a line down the center of the front steek between sts 3 and 4. Using a sewing machine and zigzag st, carefully sew sts 2 and 3 tog; turn and sew sts 3 and

4 tog. With a sharp scissors, carefully cut along the basting line, making sure that you don't cut through the zigzag sts. Do the same for the armhole steeks.

Sleeves

With RS facing and using smaller dpns and E, beg at center underarm, pick up and knit 66 sts evenly around armhole, pm for beg of rnd and join. Change to larger needles.

Rnds 1–13: Work 13-rnd Chart E, beg at Rnd 13 and working to Rnd 1 to match shoulders.

Rnd 14: K1A, *k1E, k1A; rep from * around. Cut E.

Dec rnd: With A, k1, ssk, knit to last 3 sts, k2tog, k1—64 sts.

Rep Dec rnd [every 4 rnds] 5 times, then [every

Chart E

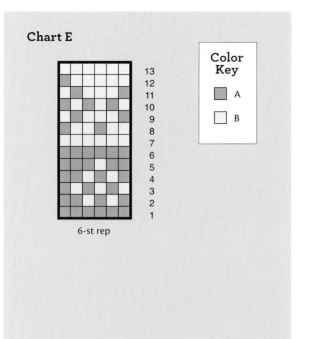

6-st rep

Color Key

▨	A
☐	B

other rnd] 5 times—42 sts.

Work even until sleeve measures 7 (7¾)"/18 (20)cm.

Cuff

Work 13-rnd Chart F.

Next rnd (turning ridge): With F, purl 1 rnd. Cut F.

Change to smaller needles and A.

Knit 14 rnds for sleeve hem.

BO very loosely. Cut yarn, leaving a very long tail.

Turn sleeve inside out and fold up hem along turning ridge.

Use tail to sew BO edge to WS of sleeve.

Buttonhole Band

Turn bottom hem up to WS along turning ridge; sew CO edge to WS.

With RS facing, using smaller needle and E, pick up and knit 68 sts along right front edge for girl (along left front edge for boy) in the first column of sts outside the steek. Pick-up rate is approx 7 sts for every 9 rows.

Row 1 (WS): P2, *k2, p2; rep from * to end.

Row 2 (RS): K2, *p2, k2; rep from * to end.

Row 3 (buttonhole row): P2, *yo, k2tog, p2, [k2, p2] twice; rep from * to last 6 sts, yo, k2tog, p2, k2.

Rows 4–5: Work in established rib.

BO loosely in rib.

Button Band

Work as for buttonhole band, picking up along opposite front and eliminating buttonholes.

Finishing

Fold cut ends of center steeks in toward inside of sweater body; sew down to body using crisscrossing sts.

Fold armhole steeks in toward body; sew down to body using criss-crossing sts.

Wash and block sweater to finished measurements. Tip: After wet sweater is positioned, whap it all over with a yardstick. This sounds strange, but it does the trick to gently flatten and smooth the knit fabric.

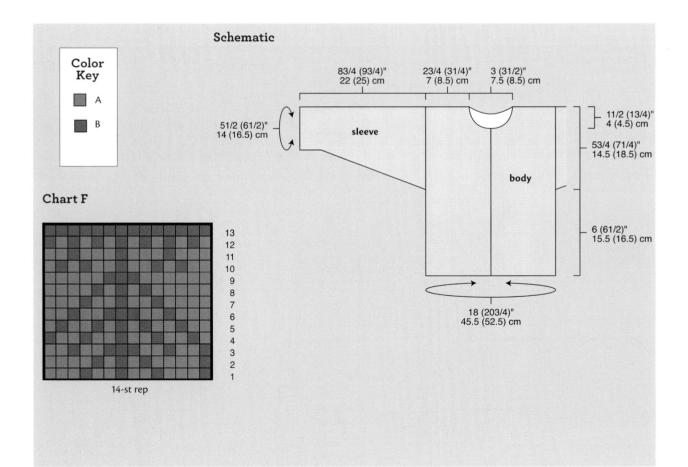

Mittens for Sven

•••

During the mass migration of Norwegians to the United States in the 1800s and early 1900s, immigrants were finding ways to blend the culture of their homeland with their new lives in American communities. One such brave soul was Berta Serina Kingestad, a single mother who settled in Illinois. In an 1889 letter sent home to Norway, Berta asked her family to send her black wool which she could spin with white American wool on a borrowed spinning wheel. She hoped to knit new woolens for her baby, Sven. Learn more about Berta and read her letters in Solveig Zempel's wonderful book, *In Their Own Words—Letters from Norwgian Immigrants*. These mittens are knit into a dense fabric for warmth, starting with a Twisted Edge at the cuff, a Norwegian knitting technique less frequently used after the 1930s.

Design by Kate Larson

Size
6-12 months

Finished Measurements
Hand circumference: 5¼"/13.5cm
Length: 5"/12.5cm
Cuff to cuff with string: 22"/56cm or desired length

Materials
[2] Dale of Norway *Falk* (DK weight; 100% superwash wool; 116yds/106m per 1¾ oz/50g ball): 1 ball each Natural #20 (MC) and Black #90 (CC)

Size 2 (2.75mm) double-pointed needles (set of 5) or size needed to obtain gauge

Tapestry needle

Gauge
30 sts and 36 rnds = 4"/10cm in stranded 2-color St st.
Adjust needle size as necessary to obtain correct gauge.

Special Techniques

Twisted Edge Cast-On

This interesting edge is worked over 2 rounds: Steps 1–4 create stitches with a variation of long-tail cast-on, Step 5 joins the rnd, and Step 6 is a round worked in twined purl.

1. Measure out a 1½ yd/1.5m tail. Hold yarns as for long-tail cast-on, with tail end over left thumb and yarn leading to ball over index finger. Tension these yarns with other fingers at palm. Using right hand, put needle under yarn stretched between thumb and finger. Right thumb holds this yarn against needle to create Joining Stitch, which is not included in stitch count.

2. While still holding yarn against needle, move needle down and toward you. Needle tip moves upward, underneath both yarns on left thumb and down through the loop on the thumb.

3. Needle moves back toward you, and then over other yarns to grab yarn on index finger from right to left.

4. Needle once again moves toward you, and then up through the loop on thumb. Drop loop on thumb and tighten new stitch. Repeat Steps 2–4 until cast-on stitches are completed, plus Joining Stitch.

5. Prepare to join to work in the round by moving stitches on 4 double-pointed needles, making sure not to twist cast-on round. Keeping yarns at back of work, move last stitch created from right needle to left. On left needle, pass Joining Stitch (now second stitch on needle) over first stitch on needle and drop. Return remaining stitch back to right needle.

6. **Rnd 1:** Bring tail and working yarn to front. *Purl first stitch, dropping yarn to far left, holding in place if necessary. Bring second yarn from underneath the other to the right and purl next stitch. Repeat from *, continuing to alternate yarns counterclockwise to form twisted edge.

Pattern Notes

Mittens are worked in the round, starting with a Norwegian-style Twisted Edge Cast-On at the cuff. Mittens are connected with a striped I-cord string.

••• Instructions

Cuff

With MC, CO 36 sts with Twisted Edge Cast-On.

Rnd 1: With CC, knit.

Rnd 2: With MC, *k2, p1, rep from * around.

Rnd 3: With CC, *k2, p1, rep from * around.

Rep [Rnds 2 and 3] 4 more times.

Rep Rnd 2 twice.

Rep Rnd 1 once more and inc 4 sts evenly around—40 sts, with 10 sts on each dpn.

Hand

Work Rnds 1–21 of Chart.

Shape Top

Top shaping decreases occur on each side of the vertical bands separating the palm from the back of the mitten. Dec rnds indicated on chart are worked as follows:

Dec rnd: Following chart, *k3 in pat, ssk with MC, work in pat to 2 sts before next vertical band, k2tog with MC; rep from * once more to finish rnd—4 sts dec'd.

Rep Dec rnd 6 more times—3 sts rem between vertical bands.

Last Dec rnd: *K3 in pat, sk2p with MC; rep from * once more to finish rnd.

Cut yarns, leaving 6"/15cm ends.

Using a tapestry needle, thread yarn tails through rem sts, pull tight, and secure.

Rep for second mitten.

Mitten Chart

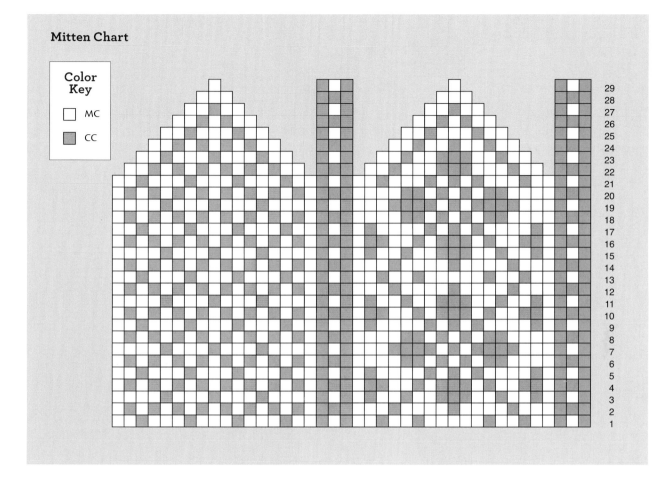

Color Key

☐ MC

▨ CC

I-Cord String

Set-up rnd: With MC, CO 4 sts. Slide sts to other end of dpn and do not turn.

Rnd 1: With CC, knit to end. Slide sts to other end of the needle and do not turn.

Rnd 2: Using MC (hanging at the other end of the work), knit 4 sts. Slide sts to other end of the needle and do not turn.

Continue working Rnds 1 and 2, taking care to bring the next color to be worked from under previous color to lock yarns together and form a tight knitted tube, until piece measures 21"/53.3cm or desired length, ending on a MC rnd.

Cut both yarns, leaving a 6"/15cm tail.

Using a tapestry needle, thread the MC tail through 4 sts and pull tight.

Finishing

Position about 1"/2.5cm of one end of I-cord inside the cuff directly below one of the vertical bands, sew in place. Rep on second mitten, sewing I-cord on opposite side as first mitten for left and right hands.

Weave in all ends. Wash mittens, shape and lay flat to dry.

Felted Baby Tote Set

• • •

This felted bag is everything a new mom would want in a baby bag. It's large enough to fit all of the essentials, yet it is so stylish that she'll be happy to carry it around. The best features of this bag are the colorful options (solid or two-color), roomy exterior pockets, a fold-over flap, and an optional zip closure. Instructions for making an accessory bag and a baby-changing pad are also included.

Design by Nora J. Bellows

Finished Measurements
Baby Bag Bottom and Body: 14"/35cm wide × 6"/15cm deep × 12"/30.5cm tall.
Place Anywhere Pockets: 5"/12.5cm wide × 7"/17.5cm tall × 2"/5cm deep
Accessory Bag: 8"/20.5cm) wide × 6"/15cm tall × 3"/7.5cm deep
Changing Pad/Seat Warmer: 12–13"/ 30.5–32.5cm wide × 23–24"/57.5–60cm tall

Materials
4 Plymouth *Galway* (worsted weight; 100% wool; 210 yds/192m per 3½ oz/100g ball): Heritage Blue #175 (A) and Bark Heather #757 (B):

- *Bicolored bag with 2 pockets, strap, accessory bag, and changing pad:* 2,100 yds/1,920m (A) and 1,050 yds/960m (B)
- *Solid bag and strap:* 1,400 yds/1,280m
- *Place Anywhere Pocket:* 200 yds/220m
- *Accessory Bag:* 200 yds/220m
- *Changing Pad:* 425 yds/389m

Size 11 (8mm) 16"/40cm and 24"/60cm circular needles (or longer) or size needed to obtain gauge

Stitch markers

Tapestry needle

Sharp sewing needle and matching sewing or nylon beading thread

1 Metal Noni Label

2 [15"/37.5cm (or longer)] Noni custom YKK large-toothed zipper with 2 sliders in chocolate or desired color

3 Noni Amazing (magnetic) snaps

8–10 Noni 24mm "Big" bag feet in nickel

1 Barcelona 37"/94cm JUL handle in brown
Paper hole punch
8-5/16"/31mm double capped rivets
Rivet setters, anvil, and rubber mallet

Gauge
Pre-felted: 12 sts and 16 rnds/rows = 4"/10cm in St st.
Adjust needle size as necessary to obtain correct gauge.

••• Instructions

Baby Bag

Bag Bottom

With 2 strands of B held tog, CO 56 sts.

Row 1 (WS): Purl.

Rows 2–36: Work in St st. BO.

Body

With WS facing and B, pick up and knit as follows: *56 sts across long side, pm, 24 sts across short side, pm; rep * once, using contrast color marker for beg of rnd—160 sts.

Cut yarn. Weave in ends on WS of bag.

With RS facing, join B at beg of rnd marker (beg of a short side); knit 4 rnds.

With A, knit 1 rnd.

Dec rnd: *Ssk, knit to 2 sts before marker, k2tog, sm, knit to next marker; rep from * once—4 sts dec'd, 2 each short side.

Continue in St st and rep Dec rnd [every 12 rnds] 6 more times—10 sts each short side and 56 sts each long side after last Dec rnd.

Flap

Establish bag front, straps, and bag back/flap as described below.

Rnd 1: Removing markers when you come to them, k10 short side sts and transfer to holder; BO 56 long side sts, k10 and transfer to holder, k56 for bag flap, turn.

Row 2 (WS): Purl.

Before continuing, choose either rounded or square edge for the flap and follow the appropriate flap instructions below.

For a round-edged flap

Rows 1–59: Work in St st.

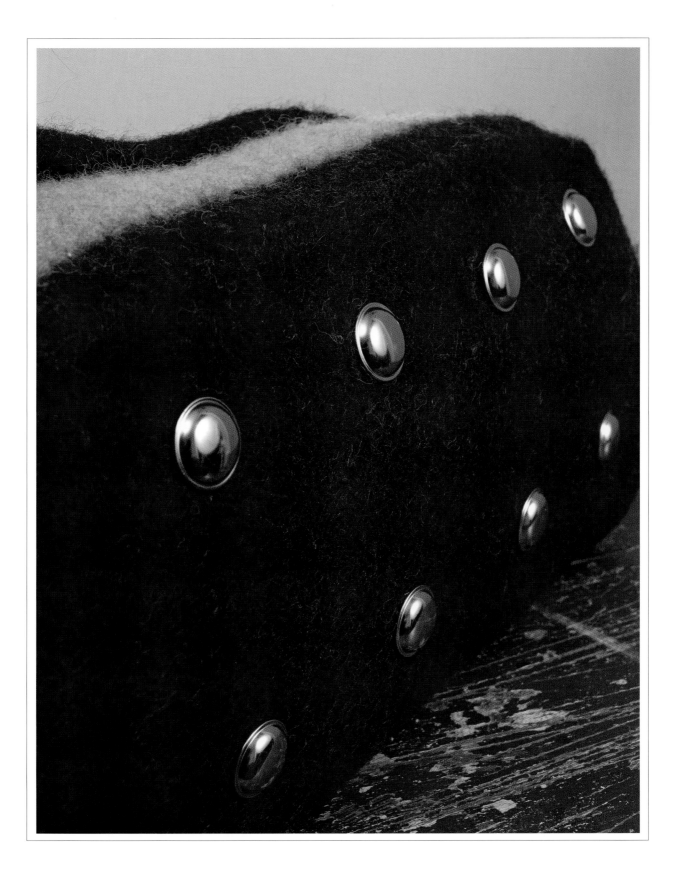

Row 60 (WS): P2, p2tog, purl to last 4 sts, p2tog, p2—54 sts.

Row 61 (RS): K2, ssk, knit to last 4 sts, k2tog, k2—52 sts.

Rep last 2 rows 3 more times—46 sts. Proceed to Edging.

For a square-edged flap

Work 68 rows in St st.

Edging

With RS facing, using a 2nd circular needle and B, pick up and knit 3 sts for every 4 rows along side edge of flap; knit across live sts on flap bottom; pick up and knit 3 sts for every 4 rows along side edge of flap, turn; using cable method, CO 3 sts.

With WS facing, work I-cord BO as follows: *K2, ssk, do not turn; sl 3 sts just worked back to LH needle; rep from * until all flap sts are bound off—3 I-cord sts rem.

Cut yarn leaving an 8"/20cm tail.

Graft last 3 sts to CO end of I-cord.

Weave in ends.

Tabs for Zipper
With WS facing and using B or color of choice, pick up and knit 56 sts along the front face of the bag opening 2 rows down from the bag BO row (you will be pullling sts through the full thickness of the bag fabric).

Cut yarn and weave ends to the WS.

With RS facing, join a new strand of B; beg with a knit row, work 4 rows in St st.

BO pwise on RS.

Rep on back face of bag opening.

Handle Tab

Transfer 10 short-end sts from holder to needle.

With RS facing, join A; work 8 rows of St st. BO.

Place Anywhere Pocket

With B, CO 22 sts. Work 12 rows in St st. BO.

With RS facing and B, *pick up and knit 8 sts along short side, pm, pick up and knit 22 sts along long side, pm; rep from * once, using contrast color marker for beg of rnd—60 sts.

Knit 3 rnds.

Change to A or color of choice; knit 10 rnds.

Dec rnd: *Ssk, knit to 2 sts before marker, k2tog, sm, knit to next marker; rep from * once—2 sts dec'd each short side.

Continue in St st and rep Dec rnd [every 14th rnd] twice more—48 sts rem after last Dec rnd.

BO pwise.

Accessory Bag Instructions

With B, CO 32 sts.

Work 18 rows in St st. BO.

With RS facing and B, *pick up and knit 32 sts along long side and 12 sts along short side; rep from * once, pm for beg of rnd—88 sts.

Knit 3 rnds.

Change to A; knit 33 rnds. BO.

Felt bag in washing machine to finished measurements.

Sew in zipper to match B or in color of choice.

Changing Pad Instructions

With A, CO 52 sts.

Work 138 rows in St st. BO.

With RS facing and B, *pick up and knit 52 sts along short side and 3 sts for every 4 rows along long side; rep from * once, turn; using cable method, CO 3 sts. Work I-cord BO as for bag flap edging.

Finishing

For best results, read entire section before felting Felting in conventional (non HE) top-loading washers. Place items to felt in separate lingerie bag(s) or zippered pillow protector(s) that are large enough not to cramp your unfelted project. Make sure any ends are woven in. Choose the smallest load size that accommodates your project and allows it to move freely—in this case, the large to extra-large load size.

Add tennis balls, sport shoes devoted to felting, or a soft canvas bag to the load to provide extra agitation and balance.

It is critical that you do not use towels or other items that will release lint onto your felt. Choose hot/cold water setting and add a tiny bit of detergent. Check often and move the bag around in the washer, making sure no set-in creases develop.

To conserve resources, turn back the agitation dial until the bag is finished felting to your liking or reaches the finished measurements here, rather than letting the machine complete multiple cycles. When your bag has reached the proper size, rinse (with no agitation or rinse in cold tap water) and spin dry. Remove and pull into shape.

Felting in HE/front-loading washers

For those with washers that cannot be opened or do not provide agitation, or those with high-speed spin cycles that might crease your bag, felt in the clothes dryer (below).

Felting in a clothes dryer

Soak your project in boiling hot water for about 10 minutes. Put in the clothes dryer. Felt just as you would in the washer: the agitation of the dryer is what causes the felting. Stay close by and check often. Once the bag has shrunk to the desired measurements, pull it into shape using the photographs on the cover to direct your efforts.

Structuring Bag with Stiffener

Use two or three sheets of Noni stiffener in the bottom of baby bag to make a mesh bottom, and then sew the mesh sheet to the bottom of the bag using a double strand of nylon beading thread and a sharp needle. Sew around the perimeter, tack down any bubbles that are present, then tack across the entire bottom.

Inserting Feet

Use a paper hole punch to create a hole for the bag foot prongs. Insert the prongs into the little hole just created and press through both the felt fabric and the bag stiffener already positioned inside the bag. Open the prongs on the inside and press down. Repeat at desired intervals, being careful to measure so that the feet are evenly placed.

Place the second sheet of stiffener inside the bag and tack in place with a sharp needle and sewing thread.

Attach Snap to the Closure Tab or Long Flap

Place the "knob" portion of snap on the flap and the "screw-in" back on the wrong side of the flap and screw into the knob front. Once this is complete, snap the magnetic "back" to the front and locate the proper position for the magnet on the bag. Press magnet prongs through felt from outside to inside, slide on washer, and open prongs. Snap closed. Open by pulling on the knob.

Attaching Straps Using Hardware and Handle Tabs

Rivet the handle ring directly to the handle tabs using a rivet-setter and anvil to set the rivets.

Sew in zipper: Pick a large-toothed plastic zipper in a matching color that is longer than the opening for your bag.

1. Fit zipper to bag: If cutting a longer zipper, use your nylon beading thread to hand-sew or machine-zigzag (in place) over the end to shorten your zipper. Trim end to ½" (1.25cm).

2. Pin one side of the zipper and sew in place: Unzip the zipper. Pin in one side at a time using large pins. Use a double-strand of nylon beading thread and sew one side in by hand using small, invisible stitches.

3. Match the other side of the zipper: Zip up the zipper and use pins to mark places on the zipper where it needs to be pinned to the other side. Do this in the beginning, middle, and end of the zipper/bag opening. Unzip the zipper again and pin entire side. Double-check that the two sides match without twisting by zipping the zipper while it is pinned. Make necessary adjustments.

4. Sew the second side of the zipper in place: Sew the second side of the zipper to the other side of the bag opening.

KNITS OF
the East

Baby Kimono Sweater

•••

Shibori Blanket

•••

Turkish Bib

•••

Amigurumi
Bird and Fish

•••

Chinese Knot
Headband

JAPANESE BEAUTY.

Baby Kimono Sweater

•••

Worked in a gorgeous lucky red color, this cute jacket will keep your little one warm while still being stylish. It's suitable for intermediate-level knitters.

Design by Melissa Leapman

Sizes
6 (12, 24) months

Finished Measurements
Chest (closed): 20 (22, 24)"/51 (56, 61)cm
Length: 10 (10½, 11)"/25.5 (26.5, 28)cm

Materials
 Cascade Yarns *220 Superwash Sport* (sport weight; 100% superwash merino wool; 136 yds/124m per 1¾ oz/50g skein): 4 (4, 5) skeins Really Red #809

Size 3 (3.25mm) straight and double-pointed needles

Size 5 (3.75mm) needles or size needed to obtain gauge

Stitch markers

2 [1⅜"/3.5cm] buttons (JHB International's #25223 was used on sample garment)

3 snaps, ½"/1.25cm

Gauge
24 sts and 40 rows = 4"/10cm in Textured pat with larger needles.
Adjust needle size as necessary to obtain correct gauge.

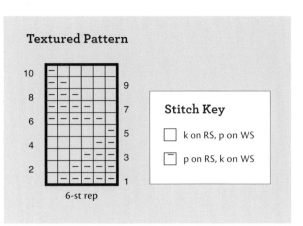

Textured Pattern

```
10 —     —
    —  —       9
8   — —  —
    — —   —    7
6   — —  —
          —    5
4
       — — —   3
2
   — — — —     1
```

6-st rep

Stitch Key

☐ k on RS, p on WS

⊟ p on RS, k on WS

Pattern Stitch

Textured Pattern *(multiple of 6 sts)*

Row 1 (RS): *P5, k1; rep from * to end.
Row 2: *P2, k4; rep from * to end.
Row 3: *P3, k3; rep from * to end.
Row 4: *P4, k2; rep from * to end.
Row 5: *P1, k5; rep from * to end.
Row 6: *K5, p1; rep from * to end.
Row 7: *K2, p4; rep from * to end.
Row 8: *K3, p3; rep from * to end.
Row 9: *K4, p2; rep from * to end.
Row 10: *K1, p5; rep from * to end.
Rep Rows 1–10 for pat.

••• Instructions

Back

With smaller needles, CO 54 (60, 65) sts.

Knit 4 rows and inc 6 (6, 7) sts evenly across last row—60 (66, 72) sts.

Change to larger needles and Textured pat; work even until piece measures 10 (10½, 11)"/25.5 (26.5, 28)cm, ending with a WS row.

BO.

Right Front

With smaller needles, CO 49 (54, 60) sts.

Knit 4 rows and inc 5 (6, 6) sts evenly across last row—54 (60, 66) sts.

Change to larger needles and Textured pat; work even until piece measures 3 (3½, 3½)"/7.5 (9, 9)cm, ending with a WS row.

Shape Neck

Dec row (RS): K1, ssk, work to end of row—53 (59, 65) sts.

Dec row (WS): Work to last 3 sts, ssp, p1—52 (58, 64) sts.

Continue in established pat and rep last 2 rows 7 (9, 11) times, then dec on RS rows only 22 (20, 20) times—16 (20, 22) sts rem.

Work even until piece measures 10 (10½, 11)"/25.5 (26.5, 28)cm.

BO.

Left Front

Work as for right front to neck shaping

Shape Neck

Dec row (RS): Work to last 3 sts, k2tog, k1—53 (59, 65) sts.

Dec row (RS): P1, p2tog, work to end—52 (58, 64) sts.

Continue in established pat and rep last 2 rows 7 (9, 11) times, then dec on RS rows only 22 (20, 20) times—16 (20, 22) sts rem.

Work even until piece measures 10 (10½, 11)"/25.5 (26.5, 28)cm.

BO.

Sleeves

With smaller needles, CO 32 (32, 38) sts.

Knit 4 rows, and on last row, inc 4 sts evenly across—36 (36, 42) sts.

Change to larger needles and Textured pat.

Inc row (RS): K1, M1, work to last st, M1, k1—38 (38, 44) sts.

Rep Inc row [every RS row] 0 (3, 0) mores times, then [every 4 rows] 8 (8, 5) times, then [every 6 rows] 0 (0, 3) times, working new sts into pattern as they accumulate—54 (60, 60) sts.

Work even until sleeve measures 4¾ (5, 5¼)"/12 (12.5, 13.5) cm, ending with a WS row.

BO.

Finishing

Block all pieces to finished measurements.

Sew shoulder seams.

Place markers 4½ (5, 5)"/11.5, 12.5, 12.5)cm down from shoulders.

Sew on sleeves between markers.

Sew side and sleeve seams.

Lower Body Edging

Front and Neckline Edging

Pick-up row: With RS facing and using smaller needles, beginning at lower right front edge; pick up and knit 18 (21, 21) sts along flat section of right front, pm, 60 (60, 63) sts along right front neck opening, 26 (26, 28) sts along back of neck, 60 (60,

63) sts along left front neck opening, pm, 18 (21, 21) sts along flat section of left front—184 (188, 196) sts.

Row 1 (WS): Knit to marker, slip marker, M1, knit to next marker, M1, slip marker, knit to end—2 sts inc'd.

Row 2: Knit.

Bind-off row: Binding off across row, knit (and BO) to first marker, M1, knit (and BO) to next marker, M1, knit (and BO) to end.

Sew 3 snaps into place between WS of left front and RS of right front.

Sew 2 buttons to RS of left front edge above snaps (see photo for placement).

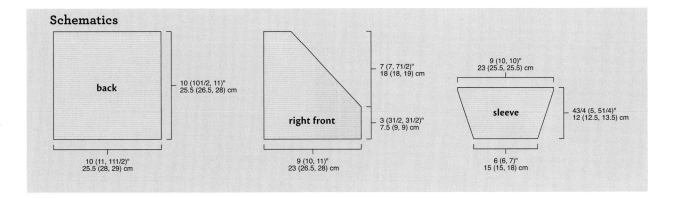

Schematics

back
10 (101/2, 11)"
25.5 (26.5, 28) cm
10 (11, 111/2)"
25.5 (28, 29) cm

right front
7 (7, 71/2)"
18 (18, 19) cm
3 (31/2, 31/2)"
7.5 (9, 9) cm
9 (10, 11)"
23 (26.5, 28) cm

sleeve
9 (10, 10)"
23 (25.5, 25.5) cm
43/4 (5, 51/4)"
12 (12.5, 13.5) cm
6 (6, 7)"
15 (15, 18) cm

Shibori Blanket

•••

The repeating pattern of shibori fabric was used as the inspiration for the semi-symmetrical pattern in the baby blanket. The suggested yarn is a soft machine-washable wool blend.

Design by Sue Flanders

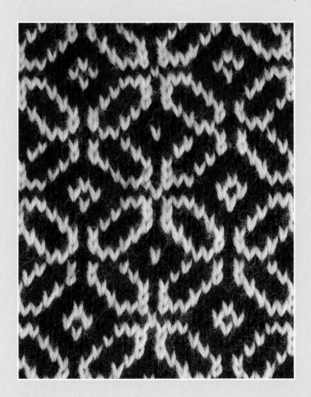

Finished Measurements
32 × 42"/81.5 × 103cm

Materials
4 Berroco *Vintage* (worsted weight; 50% acrylic/40% wool/10% nylon; 288 yds/266m per 3½ oz/100g skein): 3 skeins Dark Denim #2143 (MC) and 2 skeins Mochi #2101 (CC)

Size 7 (4.5mm) 36"/124cm circular needle or size needed to obtain gauge

Size 6 (4mm) circular needles (various lengths) for edges

Stitch markers

Tapestry needle

Sewing machine

Gauge
20 sts and 20 rnds = 4"/10cm in stranded 2-color St st with larger needle.
Adjust needle size as necessary to obtain correct gauge.

Pattern Notes

The blanket is worked in the round. Five extra steek stitches are added between the beginning and ending of each round for cutting the blanket open. The steek stitches are sewn with a sewing machine to stabilize them, and then cut. The borders are then completed and sewn down over the cut edges.

Special Abbreviation

CDD (Centered Double Dec): Sl 2 sts as if to k2tog, k1, pass the slipped sts over.

Blanket Chart

14-st rep

12
11
10
9
8
7
6
5
4
3
2
1

Color Key

A (filled)
B (empty)

••• Instructions

Blanket

With larger circular needle and MC, CO 178 sts; mark beg of rnd and join, taking care not to twist sts.

Knit 2 rnds with MC.

Set-up rnd: K2 MC, pm; join CC and work Blanket Chart to last 7 sts, pm, k2 MC, pm, [k1 MC, k1 CC] twice, k1 MC. These last 5 sts are the steek sts (see Pattern Notes).

Continue in established pattern, working 12-row chart 17 times, then rep Row 1.

Knit 2 rnds with MC.

Finishing

Set sewing machine to small sts. Place knitted tube under the machine foot and sew along the center of 1 CC column of steek sts from edge to edge, then turn and sew back along the center of the other CC column of steek sts. Rep 3 times. It is important not to sew the "ladders" between the sts, down the center of a st. This will make a much stronger steek.

Cut piece down the center MC column of sts between the machine-stitched columns.

Edging

Note: Use additional circular needles as needed to get around the entire edge of the blanket.

With RS facing, using smaller circular needles and MC, beg in center of one edge, pick up and knit 1 st for each row and 1 st for each st around blanket, using waste yarn to mark each of the 4 corner sts. Mark beg of rnd and join.

Rnd 1: Purl.

Rnds 2–4: *Knit to 1 st before marked corner st, M1R, k1, M1L; rep from * 3 more times, knit to end—2 sts inc'd each corner, each rnd.

Rnd 5 (turning ridge): Purl.

Rnds 6–9: *Knit to 2 sts from marked corner st, CDD; rep from * 3 more times, knit to end—2 sts dec'd each corner, each rnd.

BO loosely.

Fold edge to WS along turning ridge; with tapestry needle and MC, sew to WS.

Weave in ends. Block.

Turkish Bib

•••

Being part of the Silk Road, Turkey has a rich textile history that has long inspired designer Elanor Lynn—she recalls the vintage oriental carpets that covered the floors of her childhood cabin in Vermont and notes that knitting is generally thought to have originated in the Arabic world. This regal bib features her variation on an "almond" pattern, that dates from the mid–nineteenth century. Note the subtle detail of how the leaf motif alternates from right to left, resulting in a lack of an obvious center line. You might also notice that the almond motif appears complete only once. The garter stitch edge is cleverly used to counteract the curl of stockinette stitch. You can make a larger size bib by using a larger needle with the same yarn or even a DK or worsted weight on size 2 (2.75mm) or size 3 (3.25mm) needles.

Design by Elanor Lynn

Finished Measurements
6½"/16.5cm wide × 7¼"/18.5cm high

Materials
Cascade Heritage (fingering weight; 75% superwash merino wool/25% nylon; 437yds/400m per 3½ oz/100g skein: 1 skein each: Red #5607 (A), Moss #5612 (B), Denim #5604 (C)

Size 1 (2.25mm) needles or size needed to obtain gauge

⅞" (2.2cm) button

Tapestry needle

Gauge
36 sts and 44 rows = 4"/10cm in 2-color stranded St st.
Adjust needle size as necessary to obtain correct gauge.

Pattern Notes

Chart is worked in Stockinette stitch and borders are worked in garter st with A.

Colorwork is worked using both stranded and intarsia methods. Work center chart using stranded method and work borders with separate balls of A.

Outer borders and neckband are shaped using short rows.

Note: Color pattern is deliberately off-center.

••• Instructions

Bottom Border

CO 18 sts.

Row 1 and all WS bottom edge rows: Knit.

Row 2 (RS): K1, M1, knit to last st, M1, k1—20 sts.

Row 4: K1, M1, pm, knit to last st, pm, M1, k1—22 sts.

Row 6 (Inc row): Knit to marker, M1, sm, knit to marker, sm, M1, knit to end—24 sts.

Rep Inc row [every RS row] 5 more times, ending with a WS row—34 sts. Remove markers.

Set-up row (RS): K8A, M1 with A; work Row 1 of chart pat across center 18 sts; M1 with A, k8A.

Next 17 rows: Rep Set-up row and cont chart pat, working new sts into charted pat—72 sts with 9 border sts each side in A and 54 charted center sts.

Maintaining border sts in garter st with A and center sts in St st following chart, work 2 rows even, ending Row 20 of chart.

Shape Borders

Short-Row Set 1: K2, w&t, k2.

Short-Row Set 2: K3, w&t, k3.

Short-Row Set 3: K4, w&t, k4.

Short-Row Set 4: K5, w&t, k5.

Short-Row Set 5: K6, w&t, k6.

Next row (RS): K9A, work chart Row 21, k9A.

Rep Short-Row Sets 1–5 on other side.

Next row (WS): K9A, work chart Row 22, k9A.

Work 28 rows even, ending with chart Row 50.

Add center top border as follows:

Next 2 rows: K9A, work 18 sts following chart; join new ball of A and k18; work 18 sts following chart, k9A.

Center Color Chart

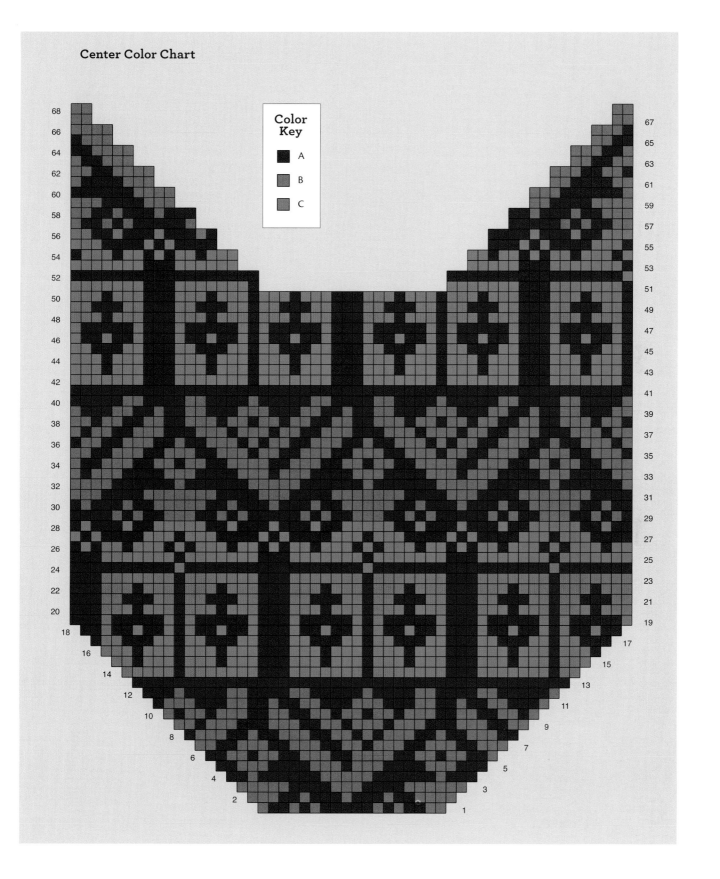

Color Key

■	A
■	B
■	C

Next 2 rows: K9A, work 16 sts following chart; k22A; work 16 sts following chart, k9A.

Next 2 rows: K9A, work 14 sts following chart; k26A; work 14 sts following chart, k9A.

Shape Neck

Row 1: (RS): K9A, work 12 sts following chart, k8A, join new ball of A and BO center 14 sts, k8A, work 12 sts following chart, k9A

Rows 2–13: Working both sides at once, shape neck as follows: K9A, work chart to 8 sts before neck, k8A, BO 2 sts, k8A, work chart to last 9 sts, k9A. *Note: When chart Row 60 is complete, continue with A only.* When neck shaping is complete, 17 A sts rem at each side.

Button Tab

Continue on the right neck sts only, leaving left neck sts at rest on needle.

Knit 5 rows.

BO 1 st at beg of next 6 WS rows—11 sts rem.

Knit 1 row.

BO. Cut yarn.

Neckband

Row 1 (WS): BO 2 sts, knit to end—15 sts.

Knit 4 rows.

BO 1 st at beg of next 6 RS rows—9 sts.

Knit 1 WS row.

Rep Short-Row Sets 1–5.

Knit 2 rows.

Rep Short-Row Sets 1–5.

Knit 36 rows.

Rep Short-Row Sets 1–5.

Knit 2 rows.

Rep Short-Row Sets 1–5.

Knit 18 rows.

Buttonhole row 1 (RS): K3, BO 5, k1.

Buttonhole row 2: K2, CO 6 sts using cable CO; slip last CO st to LH needle and k2tog with next st, k1.

Next row: K7, k1-tbl, k1.

Knit 5 rows.

Next 6 rows: K2tog, knit to end—3 sts.

BO.

Finishing

Weave in ends. Block.

Sew button to Button Tab.

Amigurumi Bird and Fish

• • •

Amigurumi is the relatively recent Japanese art of knitting or crocheting stuffed dolls and animal friends. The bird was inspired by *The Partridge Family* TV series and other vintage stylized bird representations. Fish are also an evocative symbol in many cultures. Both birds and fish represent movement (flying and swimming), and so the same tail structure is used for both animals in these designs. Since they use such a small amount of yarn, you might knit an entire flock or school from your stash. Rather than using polyester fiber filling, recycle your old socks by cutting them into ¼"/.5cm strips. By doing so, you're not only repurposing a used item, but creating a more moldable figure with better weight.

Designs by Elanor Lynn

Finished Measurements
Bird: 2"/5cm wide; 6¾"/17cm tall
Fish: 1¾"/4.5cm wide; 6¾"/17cm tall

Materials

[4] Cascade Yarns *Pure Alpaca* (light worsted weight; 100% baby alpaca; 220 yds/200m per 3½ oz/100g skein): Pacific #3049, Christmas Red #3002, Irlande #3019, and Magenta #3036

Cascade Yarns *Superwash* (light worsted weight; 100% superwash wool; 220 yds/200m per 3½ oz/100g skein): Daffodil #821

Size 1 (2.25mm) double-pointed needles or size needed to obtain gauge

Tapestry needle

Gauge
28 sts and 56 rows = 4"/10cm] in garter st.
Exact gauge is not critical for this project.

Special Abbreviation

Sssk: Slip next 3 sts 1 at a time kwise; k3tog through back loops.

Pattern Notes

Each bird or fish is made with 2 colors, A and B; only small amounts of each are needed. Mix and match colors as desired. The colors used in the samples are given in the materials list.

The fabric is deliberately very dense so that no stuffing shows through.

M1 is worked using the backward loop method.

••• Instructions

Tail (Bird and Fish)

With A, CO 14 sts.

Preparation row (WS): Knit.

Row 1 (RS): With A, k3; with B, k5, [k1 wrapping yarn around needle twice] 3 times, [k1 wrapping yarn around needle 3 times] 3 times.

Row 2: With B, k11, dropping extra wraps from previous row for elongated sts, turn without wrapping.

Row 3: With A, k11.

Row 4: With A, k14.

Rows 5–20: Rep [Rows 1–4] 4 times.

Rows 21–23: Rep Rows 1–3.

Row 24: With A, BO 13 sts, leaving last st on needle. Cut B.

Body (Bird and Fish)

Preparation Row (WS): With A, pick up and knit 6 sts along edge of tail—7 sts on needle.

Row 1 (RS): With B, [k1, M1] 6 times, k1—13 sts.

Row 2 and all WS rows: Knit back.

Row 3: With A, k2, M1, k1, M1, k7, M1, k1, M1, k2—17 sts.

Row 5: With B, k2, M1, k1, M1, k11, M1, k1, M1, k2—21 sts.

Row 7: With A, k2, M1, k1, M1, k15, M1, k1, M1, k2—25 sts.

Row 9: With B, k2, M1, k1, M1, k19, M1, k1, M1, k2—29 sts.

Row 11: With A, k2, M1, k1, M1, k23, M1, k1, M1, k2—33 sts.

Rows 13 and 14: With B, knit.

Shape Body (Bird only)

Work short rows with A, starting on RS.

Row 1: K2, wrap and turn (w&t).

Row 2 and all even-numbered rows: Knit.

Row 3: K3, w&t.

Row 5: K4, w&t.

Row 7: K5, w&t.

Row 9: K6, w&t.

Row 11: K7, w&t.

Row 13: K8, w&t.

Row 15: K9, w&t.

Row 17: K10, w&t.

Row 19: Knit.

Rows 20–38: Rep Rows 1–19 with A, starting on WS.

Continue Body (Fish only)

Work 18 rows in stripe pattern as established.

Shape Neck (Bird and Fish)

Rows 1 and 2: With B, knit.

Row 3 (RS): With A, k2, ssk twice, knit to last 6 sts, k2tog twice, k2—29 sts.

Row 4: With A, knit.

Row 5: With B, k2, ssk twice, knit to last 6 sts, k2tog twice, k2—25 sts.

Row 6: With B, knit.

Row 7: With A, k2, ssk twice, knit to last 6 sts, k2tog twice, k2—21 sts.

Row 8: With A, knit.

Row 9: With B, k2, ssk twice, knit to last 6 sts, k2tog twice, k2—17 sts.

Row 10: With B, knit.

Bird only:

Rows 11, 12, 15, and 16: With A, knit.

Rows 13, 14, 17, and 18: With B, knit.

Shape Head (Bird and Fish)

Work short rows with A, beg on RS.

Rows 1 and 2: Knit to last 3 sts, w&t.

Rows 3 and 4: Knit to last 4 sts, w&t.

Rows 5 and 6: Knit to last 5 sts, w&t.

Rows 7 and 8: Knit to last 6 sts, w&t.

Rows 9–12: Knit to last 7 sts, w&t.

Rows 13 and 14: Knit to last 6 sts, w&t.

Rows 15 and 16: Knit to last 5 sts, w&t.

Rows 17 and 18: Knit to last 4 sts, w&t.

Rows 19 and 20: Knit to last 3 sts, w&t.

Bird only:

Rows 21 and 22: With A, knit.

Fish only:

Row 21: Ssk twice, sssk, k2tog twice, sssk—9 sts.

Row 22: K6, sssk—7 sts.

Row 23: Ssk, sssk, k2tog—3 sts.

Row 24: Sssk, break yarn and draw through final st.

Beak (Bird only)

Rows 1 and 2: With B, knit.

Row 3: With A, k1, ssk, knit to last 3 sts, k2tog, k1—15 sts.

Row 4: With A, knit.

Rows 5–14: Continue decreasing on RS rows in established stripe pat until you have 5 sts.

Row 15: With B, ssk, k1, k2tog—3 sts.

Row 16: With B, p3tog. Cut yarn and fasten off.

Fin (Fish only)

Make 2

With A, CO 11 sts.

Preparation row (WS): Knit.

Row 1 (RS): With A, k3, with B, k2, (k1 wrapping yarn around needle twice) 3 times, (k1 wrapping yarn around needle 3 times) 3 times.

Row 2: With B, k8, dropping extra wraps from previous row for elongated sts; turn without wrapping.

Row 3: With A, k8.

Row 4: With A, k11.

Rows 5–12: Rep [Rows 1–4] twice.

Rows 13–15: Rep Rows 1–3.

Row 16: With A, BO 14 sts.

Finishing

Fish only: Sew fins to each side of fish as shown in photo.

Both Bird and Fish: With RS facing and A, and working from head to tail, sew seam, inserting stuffing as you go.

Chinese Knot Headband

•••

The design of this headband is focused around the Chinese Good Luck Knot.
Chinese knotting is a traditional textile practice that is said to have begun perhaps
as far back as 100,000 years ago in China. The practice has both spiritual meaning
and practical purpose and is often found within Chinese art. The Good Luck Knot
begins with a single cord that symbolizes good luck, which is then locked for all time
into the knot. In this pattern, the knitter will learn how to tie a Chinese Good Luck
Knot. The headband can be knit for any size head—from tiny baby to adult.
The headband is knit in a stitch that has elements found in the Good Luck Knot.
With the knot and the headband pattern,
this headband will bring double good luck!

Design by W. J. Johnson, Saga Hill Designs

Sizes
0–3 (3–12, 12–24, 24–36) months

Finished Measurements
Width: 1½"/4cm
Length: 12 (13¾, 15, 17)"/30.5 (35, 38, 43)cm
Be sure to measure the baby's head since
these sizes are "average" not "specific."
*Subract 1–2" (2–5cm) for negative wearing
ease.*

Materials
 Cascade Yarns *Heritage Silk* (fingering
weight; 85% superwash merino
wool/15% cultivated silk; 437 yds/400m
per 3½ oz/100g skein): 1 skein red #5607

Size 2 (2.75mm) 16"/40cm circular or straight
needles, or size needed to obtain gauge

Size E/4 (3.5mm) crochet hook

Tapestry needle

Gauge
30 sts and 40 rows = 4"/10cm in pat st.
*Adjust needle size as necessary to obtain
correct gauge.*

Pattern Notes

The headband is worked flat, then the ends are sewn together to form a loop. The Good Luck Knot is a crochet chain that is knotted, then sewn onto the finished headband.

Pattern Stitch (*multiple of 3 sts + 1*)
Row 1 (RS): P1, *k2, p1; rep from * to end.

Row 2: K1, *yo, k2, pass the yo over the 2 knit sts, k1; rep from * to end.

Rep Rows 1 and 2 for pat.

••• Instructions

CO 91 (103, 112, 127) sts.

Work pat st until piece measures 1½"/4cm or desired width, ending with a WS row.

BO in pat.

Cut yarn, leaving an 8"/20cm tail.

Use tail to sew ends together to form loop.

Weave in ends.

Chinese Good Luck Knot
Leaving a 6"/15cm tail, crochet a chain 24"/61cm long. Cut yarn, leaving a 6"/15cm tail and fasten off.

Tie the 2 tail ends together tightly to make a continous loop. You will later use the tails to secure the knot to the headband. Follow the diagram to learn how to tie a Chinese Good Luck Knot.

How to Tie Knot

To keep in mind while making the Chinese Good Luck Knot: When making the first 4 loops, be sure they are all the same size. Pay attention to the diagram to see where the loop knot and tails should be placed, since the tails will be used to attach the knot to the headband. When making the first set of loops, gently pull all loops so the next set of 4 are equal in size. After making the first set of loops, you will repeat the same loop–folding process for the second set. Then the knot will be adjusted to look like the final drawing, with 4 small loops appearing between the larger 4 loops.

Use the tail ends of the crocheted cord (which should be hanging within the center knot if the knotting instructions were followed) to sew the knot to one of the headband ridges. Secure the knot with several whipstitches and weave in ends on the wrong side of the headband. (I chose to attach it to a ridge just a few ridges over from the center of the headband.)

1

Since point 4 is the last fold, keep this bend on point 1 open so point 4 slips under it more easily.

2

4

3

Initial cord set up.
Note placement of cord tail knot.

3

4

1

2

1st knot sequence, fold over cord points in numerical order. When all folds look like drawing above, carfully pull ends to tighten knot, leaving equal loops for 2nd knot.

Final knot after tightening and all loops are adjusted.

Knitting Abbreviations

beg	begin(s), beginning
BO	bind off
CC	contrast color
cm	centimeter(s)
CO	cast on
cont	continue, continuing
dec(s)	decrease, decreasing, decreases
dpn	double-pointed needle(s)
est	establish, established
foll	follow(s), following
inc(s)	increase(s), increasing
k	knit
k1f&b	knit into front then back of same st (increase)
k1f,b,&f	knit into front, back, then front again of same st (increase 2 sts)
k1-tbl	knit 1 st through back loop
k2tog	knit 2 sts together (decrease)
k2tog-tbl	knit 2 sts together through back loops
kwise	knitwise (as if to knit)
LH	left-hand
m(s)	marker(s)
MC	main color
mm	millimeter(s)
M1	make 1 (increase)
M1k	make 1 knitwise
M1p	make 1 purlwise
pat(s)	pattern(s)
p	purl
p1f&b	purl into front then back of same st (increase)
p1-tbl	purl 1 st through back loop
p2tog	purl 2 sts together (decrease)
pm	place marker

psso	pass slip st(s) over
pwise	purlwise (as if to purl)
rem	remain(s), remaining
rep(s)	repeat(s), repeated, repeating
rnd(s)	round(s)
RH	right-hand
RS	right side (of work)
revsc	reverse single crochet (crab st)
sc	single crochet
sl	slip, slipped, slipping
ssk	[slip 1 st knitwise] twice from left needle to right needle, insert left needle tip into fronts of both slipped sts, knit both sts together from this position (decrease)
ssp	[slip 1 st knitwise] twice from left needle to right needle, return both sts to left needle and purl both together through back loops
st(s)	stitch(es)
St st	stockinette stitch
tbl	through back loop
tog	together
w&t	wrap next stitch, then turn work (often used in short rows)
WS	wrong side (of work)
wyib	with yarn in back
wyif	with yarn in front
yb	yarn back
yf	yarn forward
yo	yarn over
*	repeat instructions from *
( )	alternate measurements and/or instructions
[ ]	instructions to be worked as a group a specified number of times

Yarn Resources

Berroco
www.berroco.com

Blue Sky Alpacas
www.blueskyalpacas. com

Cascade Yarns
www.cascadeyarns.com

Dale of Norway
www.daleofnorwayyarn.com

Tahki Stacy Charles, distributor of Filatura Di Crosa
www.tahkistacycharles.com

Knit Picks
www.knitpicks.com

Koigu
www.koigu.com

Lion Brand Yarns
www.lionbrand.com

Plymouth Yarn
www.plymouthyarn.com

Quince & Co
www.quinceandco.com

Rauma
www.nordicfiberarts.com

Standard Yarn Weight System

Categories of yarn, gauge ranges, and recommended needle and hook sizes

Yarn Weight Symbol & Category Names	**0**	**1**	**2**	**3**	**4**	**5**	**6**
Type of Yarns in Category	Fingering 10-count crochet thread	Sock, Fingering, Baby	Sport, Baby	DK, Light Worsted	Worsted, Afghan, Aran	Chunky, Craft, Rug	Bulky, Roving
Knit Gauge Range* in Stockinette Stitch to 4 inches	33–40** sts	27–32 sts	23–26 sts	21–24 sts	16–20 sts	12–15 sts	6–11 sts
Recommended Needle in Metric Size Range	1.5–2.25mm	2.25–3.25mm	3.25–3.75mm	3.75–4.5mm	4.5–5.5mm	5.5–8mm	8mm and larger
Recommended Needle in U.S. Size Range	000-1	1 to 3	3 to 5	5 to 7	7 to 9	9 to 11	11 and larger

* GUIDELINES ONLY: The above reflect the most commonly used gauges and needle sizes for specific yarn categories.

** Lace weight yarns are usually knitted on larger needles to create lacy, openwork patterns. Accordingly, a gauge range is difficult to determine. Always follow the gauge stated in your pattern.

About the Designers

Myra Arnold began knitting at her mother's feet, making slippers for herself and as gifts for relatives. She also knit Barbie doll clothes and dishrags. Upon reaching a certain age, around high school, she decided that knitting was just not cool. When she became a mother, knitting was not necessary because there were already two grandmothers to knit for the children. But when one of the grandmothers passed away, she felt the need for something productive and portable to do with her hands. As a break from the children, she learned to knit again from a local yarn shop owner, and has never stopped knitting since. This is her first published original pattern, which is a team effort with her daughter, Libby Johnson.

Nora Bellows' artful Noni bag and flower designs have earned her international acclaim. A former academic with an MFA in creative writing and PhD in English Literature, Nora began creating one-of-a-kind felted bags and felted flowers under the brand Noni in 2001. She began publishing her pattern line a few years later and Noni patterns can be found in numerous yarn stores domestically and internationally. Her work has appeared in Creative Knitting, Interweave Felt, Knitting Today, Simply Knitting, and Vogue Knitting. Her lifelike knitted flowers were recently published in her first book Noni Flowers. She teaches workshops across the country

Donna Druchunas is the author of numerous books, including *Successful Lace Knitting: Celebrating the Work of Dorothy Reade, Ethnic Knitting Exploration: Lithuania, Iceland, and Ireland,* (Martingale, 2010) and *Arctic Lace: Knitted Projects and Stories Inspired by Alaska's Native Knitters* (Nomad Press, 2006). She spent four months this year traveling in Europe teaching knitting workshops and doing research for her next book, which will be about knitting in Lithuania. Visit her website at www.sheeptoshawl.com.

Sue Flanders has been designing knitwear for more than twenty years. Her patterns have appeared in many publications, including *Interweave Knits, Knitter's Magazine, Cast-On* and in two books by Melanie Falick, *Knitting America* (Artisan, 1997) and *Kids Knitting* (Artisan, 2003). She is coauthor of *Norwegian Handknits: Heirloom Designs from Vesterheim Museum* (Voyageur Press, 2009) and *Swedish Handknits: A Collection of Heirloom Designs* (Voyageur Press, 2012).

Libby Johnson lives with her husband, three young sons, cats, rabbits, fish, and other good friends in urban St. Paul, Minnesota. She reads voraciously, homeschools the kids, keeps a big kitchen garden, and loves to bike and canoe. Sunday afternoons often find her bent over a knitting project with her mother Myra, at the picnic table in summer, and before the fireplace most other seasons.

Wendy J. (W. J.) Johnson carries on a love of knitting that was sparked by her Swedish grandmother—a woman who was known to share her love of knitting with women in her rural community. Wendy's ambition is to similarly share the rich history and traditions of Swedish knitting with others, as she has done in the Swedish Fisherman's Hat pattern and in previous Knitting Around the World books, including *Knitting Socks from Around the World* (a pair of Swedish twined socks), *Knitting Scarves from Around the World* (a scarf inspired by Swedish Lovikka design), and within patterns in her own book *Yarn Works: How to Spin, Dye, and Knit Your Own Yarn*. The Chinese heritage of Wendy's goddaughter inspired her Chinese Knot Headband. She's the creative designer for her fiber arts company, Saga Hill Designs.

Kate Larson loves using fiber arts as a bridge between her passions for art and agriculture. Her fiber journey has led her to a year of study in England, a degree in Environmental Soil Chemistry, a tour of Estonian textile traditions, and back to the farm where her family has lived for six generations. She keeps an ever-growing flock of Border Leicester sheep and teaches handspinning and knitting regularly in central Indiana and around the country. Kate has published articles and designs in *Spin-Off Magazine* and is a regular contributor to the Spinner's Connection blog at spinningdaily.com. You can find her at www.katelarsontextiles.com.

A prolific designer, Melissa Leapman is the author of several bestselling knitting and crocheting books. Recent titles are *Hot Knits* and *Cool Crochet* (Watson-Guptill, 2004 and 2005), as well as the popular *Cables Untangled* and *Continuous Cables* (Potter Craft, 2006 and 2008). Her newest releases include *Color Knitting the Easy Way* and *Mastering Color Knitting*, (Potter Craft, 2010) and the must-have *Stash Buster Knits* (Potter Craft, 2011).

Three years ago, Elanor Lynn relocated from Brooklyn, New York, to Hollywood, California. Since then, she's been knitting lots of palm trees into tapestries. She's currently exploring "handwritten" fonts in text-based work.

Heather Ordover began in theater, moved to film, then ran away to teach English. Over the past seven years, she has combined all of that with her love of fiber arts to produce the podcast *CraftLit* and create the *What Would Madame Defarge Knit?* pattern book series (Cooperative Press, 2011). She knits, teaches, writes, records, and rolls around with her kids in Northern Virginia.

Kristin Spurkland learned to knit from her roommate, Sophie, in her freshman year of college. In 1998, she received her degree in apparel design from Bassist College in Portland, Oregon, and decided to pursue a career in knitwear design. She has been designing ever since. Kristin is the author of four books, including *The Knitting Man(ual)* (Ten Speed Press, 2007).

Candace Eisner Strick is an internationally known knitwear designer, teacher, and author. She has written seven books, her latest being *Strick-ly Socks*. She has contributed to all major knitting magazines, as well as book compilations, and can be found teaching all over the country at knitting events. Her line of patterns under the name of Strickwear can be found at the Ravelry store, as well as in numerous retail yarn shops. A former cellist, she lives in rural Connecticut with her husband and rescue-wonder-rabbit.

Nancy J. Thomas has recently retired from a long career in the knitting industry beginning as a magazine editor for *Knitter's Magazine* and *Vogue Knitting*. She was instrumental in the launch of *VK* in 1982. Nancy was also creative director for several yarn companies including Lion Brand, Tahki Stacy Charles and Red Heart Yarns. She is an author, teacher, and stylist. She has had a lifelong interest in all needlecrafts that began when her grandmother taught her to knit as a child.

Index

More books on knitting!

Knitting Clothes Kids Love
978-1-58923-675-2

Amigurumi Knits
978-1-58923-435-2

Knitting 101
978-1-58923-646-2

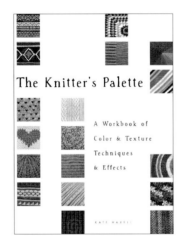

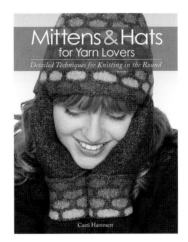

The Knitter's Palette
978-1-58923-730-8

Mittens & Hats for Yarn Lovers
978-1-58923-575-5